Beyond the Grave

Other Jack Fitzgerald books from
Creative Book Publishing

Ask your favourite bookstore or order directly from the publisher.

Creative Book Publishing
P.O. Box 8660
36 Austin Street
St. John's, NL
A1B 3T7

phone: (709) 722-8500
fax: (709) 579-7745
e-mail: books@rb.nf.ca
URL: www.nfbooks.com

Please add $5.00 Canadian for shipping and handling and taxes on single book orders and $1.00 for each additional book.

Beyond the Grave

From Crime
to Eternity

CREATIVE PUBLISHERS

St. John's, Newfoundland and Labrador
2002

©2002, Jack Fitzgerald

Le Conseil des Arts | The Canada Council
du Canada | for the Arts

We acknowledge the support of The Canada Council for the Arts for our publishing program.

We acknowledge the financial support of the Government of Canada through the Book Publishing Industry Development Program (BPIDP) for our publishing program.

Cover Design: Maurice Fitzgerald
∞ Printed on acid-free paper

Published by
CREATIVE PUBLISHERS
an imprint of CREATIVE BOOK PUBLISHING
a division of Creative Printers and Publishers Limited
an Opti-Press Inc. associated company
P.O. Box 8660, St. John's, Newfoundland A1B 3T7

First Edition
Typeset in 12 Point GoudyOlSt

Printed in Canada by:
ROBINSON-BLACKMORE PRINTING & PUBLISHING

National Library of Canada Cataloguing in Publication

Fitzgerald, Jack, 1945-
        Beyond the grave : from crime to eternity / Jack Fitzgerald.
ISBN 1-894294-54-8

        1. Newfoundland and Labrador--History--Anecdotes. 2. Ghosts--Newfoundland and Labrador. 3. Murder--Newfoundland and Labrador--History. 4. Curiosities and wonders--Newfoundland and Labrador. I. Title.

FC2161.8.F557   2002   971.8   C2002-905094-4
F1122.6.F57   2002

DEDICATION

For more than a decade, Josh, a black Labrador Retriever, stood side by side with his master Eldred Crane and together the magnetic two attracted a small army of friends. Just about every bus-driver in the City knew Josh because with his master he travelled the bus system several times a day, every day of the week. Hundreds of people who enjoy the surroundings of Quidi Vidi Lake in the summertime got to know him when they encountered Eldred and Josh in their daily walk around the lake. Hundreds, perhaps thousands got to know him or at least recognize him as he dutifully lay near his master's side in the hallway near the main entrance at the Village Shopping Centre where his master sold tickets daily for a charitable organization. To all the tenants at Regency Towers it became a daily joy to encounter their neighbours Josh and Eldred in the lobby of the building

Just days after the Regatta of 2002, it was obvious to all that Josh was not his usual self. The bounce and enthusiasm he so often displayed at any sign of affection shown him was gone. We soon learned that Josh was suffering from a serious illness.

Josh was especially blessed in his final days. He had a master who never hesitated to reward Josh's loyalty and work and spared no expense in seeking the finest medical care available. When doctors in St. John's sadly advised that they could not diagnose Josh's sickness and special medical equipment was needed, Eldred wasted no time in getting him to the Veterinary Hospital at Prince Edward Island where for several days medical doctors worked over him.

Unfortunately, Josh was suffering from a fatal disease. However, his master was able to return to him the comfort and support Josh had shown him during his lifetime. Along with giving Josh the best of care, Eldred remained at his side to comfort him, thus enabling Josh's final days to be passed in a much less stressful and comforting environment. Many lives have been enriched through the frequent encounters with Josh and his life and service to his master warrants being remembered.

TABLE OF CONTENTS

BEYOND THE GRAVE

CRIME FIGHTING GHOSTS

STORIES OF THE SUPERNATURAL MAKE THE HEADLINES

BURIED ALIVE STORIES

GHOST STORIES

JUSTICE

NEWFOUNDLAND MURDER AND MYSTERIES

BEYOND THE GRAVE

In the gas-lit city of nineteenth century St. John's, ghosts, demons and other manifestations from hell are said to have wandered the city at night. Darkly lit streets, old cemeteries and abandoned houses were avoided after dark like the plague. Outport Newfoundland had its own places and ships to avoid, especially after the setting sun and dark clouds had sucked every ounce of light from the sky. The telling of uncanny tales was a popular pastime especially on cold winter nights when families huddled around a kitchen stove or fireplace and frightened each other with stories that stood their hair on end and made their flesh crawl.

Frequently during the nineteenth and early twentieth centuries, claims of ghastly encounters were given some credibility when they were published in the legitimate news sections of local newspapers. The *Newfoundlander*, the *Evening Mercury*, the *Evening Telegram* and the *Daily News* were some of the newspapers that printed such stories. Imagine the reaction of the townspeople after reading in the newspaper of an apparition near a cemetery or an item claiming that a building was haunted. Most of the stories in this section were made known to tens of thousands of Newfoundlanders by newspapers over a hundred year period. During the mid-twentieth century, thousands of Newfoundlanders anxiously awaited each week's *Sunday Herald* to read the latest in its long running series on Newfoundland ghost stories. Unlike the stories printed in other papers during the years before, the *Sunday Herald* stories were submitted by writers from all over the province and were printed as ghost stories rather than news items. They were immensely popular and readers awaited the weekly publication with enthusiasm.

One of the most bizarre supernatural stories to make legitimate news headlines surrounded the sinking of the steamer the *Lion* off Baccalieu in 1882. That story centered around a dream that a cousin of the *Lion*'s captain had during the same hours the vessel faced tragedy.

The executions of murderers always sparked a round of ghost stories. The execution of Catherine Snow sparked many tales of sightings of her spirit; the trial of Patrick Geehan for murder had sworn evidence of a witness who claimed he met the murder victim: after the victim had died.

There are many tales of people being buried alive and even one story of a murder victim coming back from the dead to solve her own mysterious murder. The owner of a house on Murphy's Range, LeMarchant Road, in the 1950s initiated a law suit against the man who sold him the house. The basis for the suit was that the owner knew the house was haunted when it was sold.

One of the factors the stories in this section have in common with each other is that at one time or another in our history, each story was known to tens of thousands of people. They were made known and preserved thanks to our earlier newspapers. Some have an air of credibility, others seem like tall tales. Yet there was a time when most of these stories were accepted as the gospel truth by hundreds, perhaps thousands of Newfoundlanders. Because of this they have become a valuable part of our heritage and must be preserved.

DREAM FORETOLD DISASTER

The dream of a Catalina woman during the early morning hours of Old Christmas Day, January 6, 1882, caused a stir across Newfoundland and was even reported as news in the *Evening Mercury* under the headline 'Extraordinary Dream.' What made the dream so remarkable was that the woman had a vision of a Newfoundland sea disaster that was taking place in waters off Baccalieu at the same time as the dream was taking place.

When details of the dream were made public, they sparked much public interest and even warranted editorial comment in the *Evening Mercury*. It reported that the Catalina lady awoke from her sleep frightened, crying and with terror in her eyes. When her husband asked what was wrong she described the terrible dream she had which seemed so real it left her shaking even after she awoke.

In the dream she saw the steamer *Lion* moving slowly through Baccalieu Tickle. Captain Patrick Fowler, her cousin, stood on the bridge. Without warning there was a horrible explosion and Captain Fowler was, ". . . hurled from the bridge, his head blown from his body and the steamer appeared to sink in a moment with all on board." (*Evening Mercury*, January 27, 1882).

Several days after the tragedy the *Evening Mercury* reported on the event under the headline, "TERRIBLE DISASTER—Loss of the Steamer *Lion* and all on board." The story read:

> A telegram was received yesterday by W. Grieve and Co. owner stating that the fragments of two boats having on them the name *Lion* had been picked up. Also the dead body of Mrs. Cross, a passenger. The disaster

must have happened on Friday morning (Old Christmas Day), and the night had been perfectly calm and fine. The steamer *Cabot* will leave this evening to proceed down to Baccalieu Tickle in order to ascertain if possible the fate of the steamer *Lion*.

Within days after the tragedy, a St. John's man brought a copy of a letter he received from a friend at Catalina who described in detail the wife's dream of the *Lion* disaster. It was remarkable because the dream took place before it was known there was a tragedy. The *Evening Mercury* noted, "The writer we are assured, is a man of respectability and intelligence, whose veracity cannot be doubted." The newspaper described the dream as, ". . . one of the most remarkable on record." The letter read:

> This was a sad affair that of the boiler explosion of the *Lion*. On Old Christmas morning, about a half hour before daylight, my wife woke me in a fit of crying, telling me that she was dreaming that she saw the *Lion* steaming along very slowly in Baccalieu Tickle. She was, as she thought, looking at her for some time going along very slow. All of a sudden she saw her blow up and sink immediately. She fancied she heard a noise like a cannon in her head. She also saw at the explosion her cousin, Patrick Fowler, knocked off the bridge, with his head gone from his body. That was the only man's name she mentioned. "Oh my! Oh my!" she said. "Poor fellow, my poor cousin, what a sudden death you are come to!" When she awoke she said, "Oh, oh my God! Pat Fowlow won't go to the ice this spring in the *Lion*, for she has just blown up and sunk in an instant—all hands gone, himself killed and fell backwards off the bridge with his head gone."

I told her to hold her nonsense and go to sleep, and told her Pat was home a week ago with the steamer, but all of no use to tell her that. He is not home, she says, but he is gone to his long home, gone through the steamer's boiler bursting, killing him and sinking the steamer to the bottom. She says the side blew out of the steamer at the explosion and she sunk at once. I dare say if I had paid particular attention to her, and had not spoken so roughly, I might have heard more.

The *Mercury*'s editorial observed,

It is difficult to account for it on natural principle. Had the vessel been over-due, or any anxiety felt regarding her safety, then a troubled and anxious heart may have given rise to a dream of wreck and disaster. But no anxiety could have been felt, as the vessel left St. John's only six or seven hours before the dreamer awoke and by natural means, no intelligence of her sad fate could have reached Catalina.

The editorial concluded,

The coincidence of the dream and the disaster—both happening as is stated about the same hour—is certainly startling and mysterious and would lead most people to refer it to the realm of the supernatural. Verily there are more things in heaven and earth than are dreamt of in our philosophy.

The article also wondered if there was a natural explanation for the strange episode and suggested the matter warranted careful consideration.

Decades later in 1925, a lighthouse keeper told an *Evening Telegram* reporter of a strange encounter he had several years before while fishing in Baccalieu Tickle. He recalled that as he was keeping watch late one night while anchored in the Tickle he saw, ". . . a large steamship brilliantly lit up, coming towards them. He watched it for a few minutes, and seeing it coming so near their skiff, he ran and called his uncle, but just as the uncle reached the deck, the phantom ship vanished." This was considered by this man and his shipmates to be the ghost ship of the S.S. *Lion*.

DREAM SOLVED MYSTERY OF LOST EXPEDITION

A Newfoundland sealing captain's dream lead to the discovery of a lost U.S. Arctic Expedition which was the centre of world-wide attention during the 1880s. The dream lead to the rescue of seven survivors of the Greeley expedition after several search attempts had ultimately ended in failure.

In 1881 the U.S. Government commissioned Lt. Adolphis Washington Greeley, U.S. Cavalry, to carry out exploration and observations in the Arctic. The historic expedition had several strong Newfoundland connections.

The *Proteus*, which carried the Greeley team to the Arctic, was under the command of Captain Richard Pike of Newfoundland. On August 11, 1881, the *Proteus* arrived in Discovery Harbour at Lady Franklyn Bay. The expedition was very well equipped. They carried with them three years food supplies and 140 tons of coal. During the unloading of the supplies the crew built a wooden house for the expedition team.

The *Proteus* left Greeley and his men with the intentions that they would return during the summer of 1882. However, when the return was attempted, heavy ice prevented them from getting far enough north to reach Greeley.

A second attempt was made in 1883 but met with tragedy. The *Proteus* and the USS *Yanctic* made a duel effort to reach the expedition. The *Yanctic* was stopped by the ice and the *Proteus* continued north making slow progress. The *Proteus* was crushed by the ice and sank. Captain Pike and his men escaped in life boats and travelled 800 miles to Greenland.

Efforts to reach the Greeley expedition were receiving world-wide attention. The American Government offered a $25,000 reward to anyone who could find the missing explorers. During this time a third rescue effort was organized. The Americans wanted tough ships that could withstand the powerful Arctic ice. Hence they turned to the Newfoundland sealing fleet for help. The U.S. Government paid $100,000 to lease the sealing vessel *Bear* and two other Newfoundland sealing ships; *Thetis* and the *Alert*.

The three-vessel search fleet was placed under the command of Commander Winfield Schley and two Newfoundland sealing captains; Captain Frank Ash of Trinity and a Captain Norman. The men were chosen because of their extensive experience at the seal fishery in northern ice. However, unknown to the Americans, Captain Ash had a psychic connection with the search which was about to contribute to its success.

When Captain Ash boarded the *Bear* to set out for the north, he already had etched in his mind the exact location to where the expedition could be found. His knowledge came from a dream he had the night before he boarded the *Bear*. Captain Ash saw in his dream a pile of rocks protruding from the snow, which concealed information as to where Greeley and his men could be found. Based on his dream, he outlined the path the search should follow.

In following the path, the rescuers arrived at the pile of rocks just as Captain Ash had described. Hidden among the rocks they found some of Greeley's notes and records which included directions to another cache. Again the searchers followed the directions and, after rounding a piece of high land, saw a man running towards them. He was one of seven survivors of the eighteen-man Greeley expedition.

The man lead them to Greeley and the others. One man had lost both hands and feet and a spoon had been attached to the stump of his right arm. The rescuers, after getting the survivors safely on ship, went back to exhume the others from their frozen graves to bring back to the U.S. for a proper burial.

On the return trip, the vessels stopped over at St. John's Harbour where they remained for two weeks before returning the Greeley survivors to Portsmouth, New York. Greeley died in 1935 at the age of ninety-one. He had discovered new land north of Greenland. If it had not been for the prophetic dream of a Newfoundland sealing captain, the world may have never learned of the fate of the famous expedition.

DREAM LEADS TO LOST GRAVE

Another psychic experience with a Newfoundland connection took place aboard the U.S. Coastguard vessel
Eastwind during the 1950s. The vessel had sailed deep into
the Arctic to assist in setting up radar stations. An Arctic
storm came up and the *Eastwind* got stuck in the ice.
Throughout the night a crewman was tormented by a
dream. The same dream over and over. In the dream he
saw himself being beckoned on the ice towards a small
island by a ghastly figure. He followed but would awaken in
a sweat before reaching the island.

S.S. *Eagle* outside of St. John's Harbour.

The next morning at breakfast, he was still bothered by
the dream. Soon after breakfast the storm abated and they
could see they were near a small island. While he stared
from the deck towards the barren wind-swept island, he

felt compelled to go to it. He took his camera and joined several crewmen in going to the island.

Once there, he soon found a satisfactory explanation for his weird dream. Overnight the wind had blown enough snow away to reveal a grave with the blade of a broken oar embedded into a cairn of stones. He took a picture. A few years later the picture appeared in a Boston newspaper with the caption 'Lonely Arctic Grave.' It also mentioned there was a carving on the oar, "Sacred to the memory of James Harkins, seaman, native of Perlican, Newfoundland. Age 22 - S.S. *Eagle*, September 1891."

It is believed that the *Eagle* referred to is the famous Newfoundland sealing vessel which made several whaling voyages to the Arctic. It was brought outside St. John's in the mid-1950s and sunk.

PREMONITION

William J. Lundrigan was happy to be returning to his home in Corner Brook after undergoing medical treatment at the Royal Victoria Hospital in Montreal. He boarded the ferry at Port aux Basques just before midnight on October 13, 1942. Within an hour his mood took a sudden dramatic change. His happy, cheerful mood was replaced with a dreaded feeling that something very terrible was about to happen.

Lundrigan later told reporters that he, ". . . had a premonition something was going to happen that night. I just can't explain it, but there was something ominous and foreboding that night." Soon after midnight he had fallen asleep. Within an hour he awoke in a sweat. He had a dream which had left him with a feeling of dread. Five times afterwards he tried to get back to sleep but the feeling of impending disaster prevented him from doing so.

Finally he drifted into a light sleep. At 3:45 a.m. he was startled out of that sleep by a loud explosion. For the next week newspapers across North America told the story. The S.S. *Caribou* on which Lundrigan was a passenger had been sunk by a German torpedo and sent to the bottom of the Atlantic. A week later the *Evening Telegram* ran Lundrigan's story under the heading: "*Caribou* Survivor Had Premonition of Disaster."

PRIEST'S STRANGE POWER

A very strange story took place at Shoal Bay, near Petty Harbour sometime in the 1930s. During a hot summer day, a sixteen year old boy fell from his father's fishing boat and drowned. For several days fishermen from Petty Harbour searched without success for the boy's body. In desperation the boy's father, who had not been inside a church for ten years, sought the help of Father Dean Cleary, the parish priest at Petty Harbour and pleaded with him to come to Shoal Bay and pray that the body would be found.

The priest listened intently to the man and invited him into the church to pray. Afterwards he told the man to go back to the place where the boy fell into the water at 10:00 a.m. the next morning. He added, "You will not need me there. The Lord will guide you."

That night the fisherman told his wife his feelings had changed after leaving the priest. He said he felt more at peace and was optimistic that he would find his son's body and give him a decent burial.

The next morning about twenty boats turned up for the search. Among them was the boy's father. He followed the priest's suggestion and at 10:00 a.m. found himself in the area where his son had fallen into the water. He looked down into the water and exclaimed, "Thank God!" He had discovered his son's body. He thought of the priest's words as he called for help from others to retrieve the body.

Shorty afterwards, a service was held at Petty Harbour for the boy. It was said that the father never missed a Sunday mass again.

'DEAD WATER'

During the 1920s, Newfoundland fishermen participating in the Labrador fishery were spooked by an uncanny phenomena which became widely known as the 'Dead Water.' Skipper Dan Walsh of St. John's who spent many seasons at the Labrador fishery and the seal fishery would often refer to the Dead Water as haunted waters. He believed the unexplained happenings there were caused by the lost souls of fishermen who had drowned in the area over the years.

The strange occurrence took place in waters off Stag Bay near Nain, Labrador. Every spring fishermen set out from Newfoundland ports for the Labrador fishery but the most experienced avoided the place near Stag Bay known as 'Man Rock Run.' It was in that place that the Dead Water was experienced. It was a place where, in the 1890s, a fishing vessel with a twelve-man crew went down with all hands on board. Skipper Walsh, when telling the Dead Water tale, would argue that the drowning men had cursed the area as the sea swallowed them. Regardless of why it happened, many Newfoundland fishing vessels experienced it.

Skipper Walsh described his first experience with it:

> We were steaming along at about two knots, but like many boats before us, would be stopped dead. Even though the water surrounding the boat was calm, we got a really strange feeling. No man produced force could move us. And when we stood on the deck in amazement ice would drift right by. How could that happen? What was stopping us from moving?

He added that even when the auxiliary engine was engaged the vessel would not move. "We prayed. What else could we do?" He continued, "Eventually, the spell broke and we were set free. One boat that got caught in the Dead Water tried turning in all directions but it was impossible to move."

DEAD RECLAIM THEIR GOLD

The disappearance of a 'King's Ransom' in gold at St. John's Harbour sparked many rumours including a supernatural explanation. This story is related to one of Newfoundland's most intriguing stories involving the sinking of the S.S. *Anglo Saxon* near Cape Race on April 27, 1863. There were 450 people on board and 300 drowned in the catastrophe.

Around the same time of the wreck, a fishermen named Henry Fitzpatrick of Placentia was sailing his fishing vessel to St. John's. Fitzpatrick had been fishing near Cape St. Mary's and was en-route to the city to pick up supplies. Off the shore at Renews, Fitzpatrick came upon floating wreckage from the *Anglo Saxon*. With the help of his four member crew, he brought on board many items including a large metal strong-box, locked tight with three pad locks.

Rather than open it up right there, he decided to wait until he arrived at St. John's Harbour. The strong-box was placed down on the ballast of the vessel for safe keeping. However, when Fitzpatrick and his crew went to retrieve it after arriving in the city, they were dismayed to discover that it was missing. Nobody had been on board and they had not been tied up long enough for anyone to get on board. The ship was completely searched but without success.

The *Anglo Saxon* was believed to have been carrying a 'King's Ransom' in gold destined for the United States for some purpose involved in the American Civil War. Fitzpatrick was stumped as to how it could have disappeared. Perhaps a crew member had opened it and somehow managed to get it off ship without the others knowing. Some even claimed the box carried the wealth of the ship's passengers and that the dead had come to reclaim what was theirs.

The truth was never discovered and the disappearance of the strong-box remains one of Newfoundland's many intriguing mysteries.

The *Strathella*, a 700 ton English cargo-vessel, was at the dry-dock in St. John's for several months in 1945 before supernatural claims related to the ship made newspaper headlines. Strange and unexplained circumstances relating to the ship at the time of its rescue on the North Atlantic fanned much speculation throughout Newfoundland. The *Strathella* was referred to among the public as the 'Ghost Ship' and sometimes the 'Mystery Ship.'

Stories regarding the Ghost Ship originated in the dockyard and made their way into the *Evening Telegram*. One headline in the *Evening Telegram* stated: "Mystery Trawler Undergoing Repairs." The article even compared the Ghost Ship with the legendary 'Flying Dutchman' story, ". . . which is supposed to be erratically roaming the seas and which, according to a local chronicler, was seen off the port of St. John's many years ago by the caretaker at the blockhouse (Signal Hill)."

By the time the *Strathella* made the local news two legends had spread throughout Newfoundland regarding its surrounding mystery. The first tale claimed, ". . . the trawler was found bereft of accommodations and equipment, abandoned and drifting at the caprices of the tides and winds on the Atlantic. There was neither hide nor hair of any of the crew. The story goes, she was towed to Bay Bulls and later St. John's."

The second legend mentioned, "The *Strathella* had been found by an American Coastguard-cutter drifting on the high seas. A boarding party reputedly discovered ample supplies of food on the ship but no crew."

These stories and the exaggerated claims of a ghastly presence having taken over the ship prompted many questions. Was there a rational explanation for the mystery? If not, what strange force had caused the crew to abandon ship in the North Atlantic? Why haven't any signs of lifeboats or survivors been found? Was the *Strathella* still haunted?

While public fascination with the Ghost Ship grew, workmen at the dockyard continued the work of reconversion of the vessel. By then the public believed that the *Strathella* was definitely a ghost ship and this belief was strong enough that even when the Royal Navy records revealed what had actually happened, many refused to believe it.

According to the Navy records, "The trawler had been lost from a convoy after developing both engine and wireless trouble. Tossing helplessly on the bellows, the craft drifted for six weeks until the coast of Greenland hove in view and so did a Coastguard-cutter, which towed it to a northern port. The crew was weak and gaunt for want of food and after convalescing at a shore hospital they were sent home." Not everyone accepted this explanation. After all it had the makings of a good ghost story!

About twenty years later, Sgt. Bill Bennett of the Royal Canadian Army, then living in Montreal, met an old army acquaintance from St. John's. They had lunch together and reminisced over old war-time stories and memories about St. John's. Among the tales recalled by Sgt. Bennett's friend was that of the Ghost Ship, the *Strathella*, which he referred to as Newfoundland's Flying Dutchman story.

In 1949 a reporter described the encounter of a four year old boy as, "One of the most incredible performances of a young boy's return from death." The incident took place at Spillar's Cove about four miles from Bonavista.

Greg Fleming, just four years old at the time, was sliding with his brother down over a hill close to a cliff stretching into the sea. There was a turn in the hill just before reaching the cliff and the children of the area felt safe sliding there. Unfortunately, Greg Fleming struck a patch of ice and went sliding past the turn and out over the forty-two foot cliff landing in the waters below. The bay at the time was covered with slob ice.

Greg's older brother rushed home to get help but was in such a hysterical state that he was unable to articulate what had happened. His parents sensed something terrible had taken place and they followed their son to the bay. When they realized what had happened they, with the help of others, went out in a dory to search for their son. They rowed to a place where a black spot could be seen in the ice about twenty-five feet from shore. The child's slide was lying overturned on the ice and the child's fingers could be seen grasping it.

Bernard Fleming, Greg's father, pulled him in and placed him over the gunwale of the dory and attempted artificial respiration. However, the child was frozen stiff and the father couldn't even bend young Greg's body.

While Bernard Fleming tried to help his son, friends had gone for help to the Bonavista Cottage Hospital. Dr. Forbes responded to the emergency and rushed to the Fleming house and wasted no time. Using a small axe he chopped the ice from the child's body and then peeled off the clothing with a surgical knife. By then everyone believed that Greg was dead, but Dr. Forbes did not give up. For forty-five minutes he attempted to revive Greg. And then those in the house witnessed what they believed was a miracle. Young Greg began breathing. Some people in the Bonavista area still talk about the boy who was brought back from the dead.

THE ANGLICAN CATHEDRAL MIRACLE GLASS

The Anglican parish of St. John's is the oldest Anglican parish in the world. Between 1699 and 2000 a succession of fifteen churches were built on the site of the present Cathedral. Most of these were wooden structures. Several fascinating stories are associated with the Cathedral. In 1847 Bishop Field and the Reverend Jacob Mountain left England on the *Hawk* for St. John's to officiate at the turning of the sod to build a new stone-structured Cathedral to replace the one destroyed in the 1846 fire.

The *Hawk* was blown off course in a series of Atlantic storms. While the two clergymen prayed for deliverance, the St. John's congregation anxiously awaited their arrival. They too prayed for the seemingly lost at sea clergymen but, after almost two weeks waiting, decided to proceed with the sod turning. Most felt the *Hawk* was lost at sea with all on board. The sod turning ceremony was set for May 25, 1847.

As crowds gathered at the site for the ceremony word spread that a ship was entering the harbour. It was soon identified as the *Hawk* and all on board were safe. The sod turning ceremony proceeded and the congregation gave thanks for what they believed to be God's work.

Corner of Queen's Road and Duckworth Street. (near Gallows Hill)

Although services were held as early as 1850, work on the Cathedral was not completed until 1885. Seven years later in 1892 the great fire that swept the city destroyed all but part of the structure of the Cathedral. The roof had collapsed, the nave destroyed and the walls fell. All but one stained glass window remained. The 'Resurrection,' as the stained glass was named, was dedicated to the memory of George Johnston Hayward 1798-1884. While carefully removing the window for safe keeping, a peculiar aspect was noticed by workmen and clergy. On the faces depicted in the stained glass, there were distinct tear-like drops. Authorities explained that these were caused by molten lead. However, people in the city viewed it as a miracle.

When the church was rebuilt in 1893 that same window was installed again.

Anglicans, Roman Catholics and people of all faiths in the city joined in the effort to rebuild the Cathedral. The Star of the Sea Association held a football game to raise money and Anglicans around the world contributed financially to the cause. The Cathedral was reconstructed and dedicated on June 28, 1895.

The old Anglican graveyard operated from around 1700 to the early 1800s. During this period about 6,000 people were laid to rest there. In 1759 the Gallows, which were near the eastern corner of Duckworth Street and Church Hill, were moved to Gallows Hill (corner of Bates Hill and Queens Road).

CRIME FIGHTING GHOSTS

Several unearthly stories related to the criminal history of Newfoundland went beyond the folklore type ghost stories and received the attention of the legitimate media. People were more ready to believe these ghost stories because of the credibility associated with how they came to public attention. These stories were given under oath during murder trials.

WITNESS FACE TO FACE WITH MURDER VICTIM

One of the very rare times in Newfoundland and Canadian history in which a witness in a murder case under oath swore that he had come face to face with the ghost of the murder victim took place in Newfoundland in 1872. Patrick Morrissey of Harbour Grace gave this startling testimony during the double murder trial of Patrick Geehan and Johanna Hamilton for the murder of Geehan's wife and his brother-in-law Garrett Sears. Not only was Morrissey's testimony uncanny but it was an important part of the prosecution's case and helped convict the two accused.

The double murder took place on November 20, 1871, when Geehan shot his wife then shot and bludgeoned his brother-in-law at the Geehan Farm in Harbour Grace. Johanna Hamilton helped Geehan hide the bodies and cover up the murders. (Full story in *Ten Steps To The Gallows*, Jack Fitzgerald, 1981, Jesperson Press.)

During the trial, Patrick Morrissey's incredible evidence was given and sparked ghost stories about the murder for the next several decades. According to court records, Sears had been buried about two miles from the Geehan farm. Geehan and Hamilton told neighbours that Mrs. Geehan and Sears had gone to St. John's. At the trial, Morrissey swore that he saw Sears several days after he was murdered and before the murders had been detected. He said the man had an eerie appearance which alarmed him (Morrissey).

Patrick Morrissey told the court, "I saw the man coming down the road, his face was pale, he looked queer. I got frightened. I said to myself let Garrett Sears be dead or alive, that is him." The witness said he wanted to follow Sears but his family stopped him. Morrissey continued, "When I met Geehan the next day, I asked him if that was Sears who went into his house last night." Geehan's head dropped and he answered, "Sears didn't go down the road last night . . . . unless he went down dead."

Geehan then asked Morrissey if he felt Sears could have killed his own sister. Morrissey answered, "I fell in company with a good many in my time that read a good deal. I read a good deal myself, but I never read and no man ever told me he read of the brother ever killing the sister or the sister killing the brother." He continued, "But I've heard tell of many a one that read of the husband killing the wife or the wife killing the husband. 'Farewell, now forever more.' I don't know why I said that but I did."

Another eerie story told relating to the Sears murder is that the victim was determined that his murder would not remain a secret to history. According to this story the dead man reached from the grave to reveal the murder. His body was discovered by his hand and part of his arm reaching out of his grave. This brought the police to the scene and lead to the arrest and conviction of Geehan and Hamilton.

In fact the hand reaching from the grave was true, and it did lead to the finding of the body. To quote from the story in *Ten Steps To The Gallows*, "A hand sticking out of a grave drew police attention to the pit on the Geehan family farm at Harbour Grace where the body of the slain Garrett Sears was buried. Digging through the manure and clay piled on top of the shallow grave, police didn't take long to uncover the body hidden below."

Danny Shaugharoo of Harbour Grace saw the hand reaching out of the grave and called in police. At the time there were no supernatural claims attributed to the finding. When the victim was buried, he was dragged by the feet into the grave with his hands extended above his head. It was believed that animals digging at the gravesite had uncovered enough dirt to reveal the arm and hand. However, in time the hand from the grave became a popular ghost story in the area and was even remembered in St. John's as late as the 1950s.

GHOST SOLVES MURDER MYSTERY

Did the ghost of a murdered Newfoundland girl actually solve the mystery of her own killing and cause the murderers to be brought to justice? This question was the basis of a ghost story that gripped the city of Boston for more than a decade after the murder of Annie Mullins in 1909. The people of Boston could hardly be blamed for raising the question and keeping the story alive. Liz Delurey, the key witness in the murder trial, claimed that she was forced by Annie's spirit to go to police with her evidence. Liz was the aunt of Annie Mullins.

Annie Mullins moved to Boston from St. John's around 1906 and found employment as a domestic with a professor at Harvard University. One evening, while returning home from a church service, she was dragged into a field by two men who slit her throat when she resisted their advances.

The killing received tremendous attention in the U.S. and three police departments, an investigative reporter and a hot-shot New York detective were unable to break the case. While investigators pondered the mystery, Aunt Liz Delurey was keeping a secret. She knew who killed her niece and not even the murderers knew she could identify them as the killers. Aunt Liz had decided that she would never reveal her secret. That was before the haunting started. The ghost of Annie Mullins haunted Aunt Liz; at first night after night and then even in the daytime. The hauntings were not confined to the house. When Aunt Liz went to the barn to milk the cows she would encounter the spirit of the murdered victim.

At the beginning Aunt Liz believed the hauntings were nothing more than her imagination. She had been through a lot over the previous months and perhaps it was getting to her she thought. But the hauntings became so frequent that Aunt Liz broke down and told police the secret she had kept for a whole year.

Aunt Liz's nephew, Peter Delurey and his friend Jim Manter, both of whom worked on her farm, were arrested and charged with the murder of Annie Mullins. The testimony of Aunt Liz helped convict them. (See *Rogues and Branding Irons*, Jack Fitzgerald). She told the court that on the day Annie's body was found, the two had come home around 5:00 a.m. They told Aunt Liz that a girl had been murdered and her body found in the field near the church. The two claimed they had been at the murder scene for most of the night with other spectators watching the police in action. Later that morning Aunt Liz read in the morning paper that the body had not been found until 6:30 a.m.

In her statement to police, which in court helped convict the killers, Aunt Liz explained why she came forward.

> The ghost of Annie Mullins was always there. She haunted me and tormented me until I couldn't take it anymore. Her ghost seemed always hovering about me and I got so that I couldn't go around the corner barn without expecting to see her. It got so bad I simply couldn't stand it any longer so I contacted the police. I wanted to clear Annie Mullins of the things said

about her. She was a good, pure girl. Annie and my nephew Peter went to the same church and sat in the same pew together."

Annie Mullins was the daughter of Mr. and Mrs. William Mullins of Blackmarsh Road, St. John's, Newfoundland.

THE GHOST OF THE BRASS CASTLE

Although no court case was involved in this story, it had some credibility because people in the neighbourhood of the crime knew the murder victim and were convinced his spirit haunted the area. Reports of the apparition appeared in newspapers and the story became known to thousands.

The Brass Castle was a scrap metal business on the west side of Springdale Street near the Water Street intersection. It was operated by Billy McCarthy who lived alone in the house adjoining the business. Mr. McCarthy was found murdered in the kitchen of his home on January 29, 1894. It was a brutal murder. His head was bashed in and blood was spattered all over the kitchen. The murder was never solved. (Story in detail in *Convicted* by Jack Fitzgerald.)

Wherever a murder took place in Newfoundland, particularly in the nineteenth century, it was inevitable that tales of ghastly apparitions would soon follow. The Brass Castle was no exception. Claims that the place was haunted by a spirit made the local newspapers over the following twenty-five years.

For years after the killing, people avoided the area at night and the story of the murder was kept alive by parents who told the frightening story to their children. It's not surprising then that the first sighting of McCarthy's ghost was by a little girl who lived in the home adjoining the Brass Castle. She claimed that when she looked out her bedroom window one night she saw the ghost of an old man looking back at her from the Brass Castle kitchen. She claimed the face was covered with blood and he was pointing towards a wall.

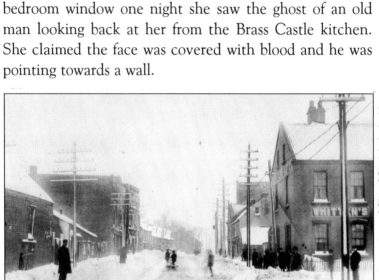

Water Street west of Springdale Street around 1907.

Another sighting was reported by a man who owned a nearby butcher shop. His description of the spectre was similar to the little girl's but he said the spirit was dressed in dripping oil clothes. Just prior to World War II the last reported sighting of the Brass Castle Ghost was made. A mother, who went into the laneway next to the Brass Castle looking for her child, ran from it screaming. She told neighbours that the ghost of old McCarthy was staring at her from the kitchen window.

The motive for the murder of McCarthy was believed to be robbery. People who knew McCarthy claimed he hoarded money. In 1940 the Brass Castle was torn down. It is said that inside the wall, where the spirit is said to have pointed, was found a strong box containing McCarthy's fortune.

CIVIL CASE BASED ON HAUNTING

A civil dispute between a home owner and the man from whom he purchased a LeMarchant Road home was based on a claim that the house was haunted. In 1945 a man purchased the three story house on Murphy's Range (a part of LeMarchant Road up to the 1960s) for $5,000. It appeared to be a good bargain for the house was well kept and in top condition. However, soon after the man and his family moved in, bizarre things began to occur.

At first, knocking noises were heard at night. Then sometimes there would be singing in the attic. Shortly after that all the usual phenomena associated with a haunted house began to happen. The owner told a reporter that, "Things got so bad we finally had to quit; the wife, and especially the children, couldn't stand it anymore." The family moved out and the story of its haunting spread around the city. While the man tried to get his money back the house remained vacant. Nobody could be found to buy or rent it. The man planned on taking the owner to court based on his claim that the owner had known the house was haunted.

Adding to the mystery of the house was the fact that in a ten year period, twenty-two people had died in the home. The deaths were confirmed to be of natural causes; two of them from old age, but the rest had been young and middle-aged people. Causes of death included heart attack, tuberculosis and cancer. Yet people found it peculiar that so many had died in the same house in a relatively short period of time.

The matter was eventually settled when the seller, to avoid public embarrassment, bought back the house for a little less than for which he had sold it. Had the matter gone all the way to court, it would have been the first and perhaps the only case in Newfoundland history based on supernatural arguments.

The house remained vacant for months after its secrets had been brought to public attention. Eventually it was sold and the family that moved in were not bothered by its eerie reputation. As a matter of fact, during house parties, the owner would remind guests that, ". . . this very living room played host to twenty-two corpses."

STORIES OF THE SUPERNATURAL MAKE THE HEADLINES

The following tales of the supernatural tell of a miraculous answer to a prayer, a haunted building and mysterious lights. Each appeared in newspapers throughout Newfoundland and became known and firmly believed by tens of thousands of people.

FIRE COULDN'T HARM THIS HOUSE

Among the strange and unusual occurrences in Newfoundland history is a remarkable event which took place during the terrible fire at Harbour Grace which destroyed most of the town in the nineteenth century. One particular home was surrounded by fire but not touched. Many believed nothing short of miraculous intervention had saved the Ross home.

High winds fanned the raging fire as it swept along Water Street destroying everything in its path. The Ross home was directly in the path of the fire. William Fleming from Bell Island was boarding at the Ross's that year. Rather than abandon the house to the oncoming flames, he cut a picture of Saint Jude from a prayer book and invited Mrs. Ross and another boarder to pray with him.

Anxious minutes turned into hours and the fire destroyed every house on both sides of the Ross bungalow, but the Ross home survived untouched by the flames. Up until the 1940s, Mrs. Ross kept that picture of Saint Jude displayed on a mantle in her home and never missed a chance to tell of her miraculous experience.

THE HAUNTED BUILDING OF DUCKWORTH STREET

Over the long history of St. John's many hauntings and ghostly appearances were believed to be real occurrences and were treated as news in the local newspapers. The following item is such a story and was reported in the *Evening Telegram* on August 9, 1879. It was headlined, "SPIRITUAL VISITATION." The newspaper reported:

A few nights ago just at the hour when graveyards yawn, a watchman, whose name we need not mention, was frightened almost, if not altogether, out of his wits, by unearthly moans and sepulchral groans emanating from a building in course of erection on Duckworth Street." (Historical records show that the Kirk, built after the original one was destroyed by fire, was under construction in 1878 and 1879 and was dedicated by Rev. L.G. McNeil, November 29, 1879. It was less than a hundred feet from the St. John's Cemetery now the Anglican Church yard fronting on Duckworth Street.)

The newspaper continued,

With nerves braced up to their utmost tension, hair erect and trembling lower extremities he moved in the direction of the 'haunted building' with a view to discover, if possible, the character of the nocturnal visitant. As he approached the structure the darkness became intense, and the noise grew deafening and still more unearthly. Shaking and quaking, he at length mustered courage to address the 'spirit' in the usual way.

The answer came: "I am the ghost of an unfortunate rum seller, eternally doomed to roam a fugitive about this mundane sphere. The misery I once caused others to suffer is now heaped upon me seven fold. I am the most unhappy spirit that ever scaled the battlements of perdition. Oh! Oh! Ohhhhhh!"

The watchman is still alive; but he has made up his mind never again to do duty in the vicinity of that building.

(*Evening Telegram*, August 9, 1879)

(The Duckworth Street Kirk was destroyed during the Great Fire of 1892. The building which replaced it has been used for a variety of purposes since that time including: hotel, private residence and restaurant. Claims of strange happenings and hauntings were being reported as recently as the last decade when it was commonly known as Victoria Station.)

Duckworth Street showing "The Kirk".

TRINITY LIGHTS

During the early twentieth century, Newfoundlanders were fascinated by supernatural stories. In the mid 1920s, the *Evening Telegram*, commenting on this interest noted,

> Perhaps the most modern mystery of the spirit world is taking place here in Trinity at the present time. About the year 1916, a very brilliant light appeared a few

miles off the narrows of Trinity. At first it was thought to be the light of an approaching ship. In fact the Fort Point lighthouse keeper was so sure of this light being of the S.S. *Prospero* that he rowed across the harbour in great haste to be at the public wharf on her arrival, only to discover later that there was no approaching ship.

The *Evening Telegram* story continued,

This mysterious 'Light Story' became known abroad and all the inhabitants of the town became nervously interested and excited fearing that it was a German submarine attempting to cut the Atlantic Cable or to attack the town. Hundreds of people watched this light, night after night and the agitation became so rife that it was reported to the authorities at St. John's and then to the Heart's Content Cable Co., only to be assured that nobody was tampering with the cable. This set the minds of the Trinity people at rest, but still the 'Mystery Light' appeared and is still appearing.

That same year, according to the story, a fisherman was on the fishing ground after dark and saw the light a few hundred yards in front of his boat. He rowed towards it, but as he neared it disappeared.

(*Evening Telegram*, 1925)

ST. JOHN'S TERRORIZED BY MYSTERY LIGHT

During the early part of the twentieth century, St. John's and nearby communities were terrorized by reports of sightings of an invisible being. This strange spectre was described as an invisible being who carried a lantern while haunting and spooking townspeople. Jim Cooper, who lived at 19 Field Street during the 1940s, recorded his knowledge of the spectre in a short story. Mr. Cooper said, "The people called it a lantern, but in reality it was an eerie and bright ball of vapour covered light."

People claimed to see the light moving across Southside Hills at night and according to Cooper there were three credible encounters with it. He said people referred to the phantom light as 'Jack-O'Lantern.' He said, "Jack O'Lantern first put in an appearance about the year 1900 and continued to appear for several years after."

Mr. Cooper wrote,

> At the time when Jack O'Lantern did his haunting, many were the questions as to what he was, his intentions, and most of all where he came from? Some said he was the devil, others that he was an invisible fairy who wanted to help the poor, but was afraid of humans and would run away when any one came near him. Most people said he was a ghost, commonly known at that time as a haunt.

Tales from that era claimed that Jack O'Lantern would be seen hanging in mid-air with not a sign of anything holding it up. Night after night he would be viewed going back and forth the Southside Hills as if looking for something. Many brave youths from the city would go to the Southside hoping to find an explanation for the light, but none were successful. They said it would be seen zig zagging across the hill; disappearing and reappearing.

Jim Cooper offered three incidents involving the mysterious figure. He stated,

A young married couple had been visiting friends and were wending their way home over LeMarchant Road. All the while they had been noticing a light that seemed to be always the same distance behind them. Suddenly the woman screamed out in terror. The ball of light was coming after them. It came with a hopping motion as if something was holding it while jumping in the air. Without hesitation they ran. Stumbling and winded, the man half dragged the woman with him. When they glanced behind the mystery light had gone.

He described a second incident at Coate's Marsh off the Ruby Line on Bay Bulls Road. Cooper claimed,

This time the light was seen on top of a post. A dozen men or more banded together to investigate, but on arriving at the marsh the light left the post and went hopping over the marsh and into the woods.

Berry pickers were common on the Southside Hill and one story tells about the time when Jack-O-Lantern led a group of berry pickers safely out of the woods. They had gone too deep in the wooded area and darkness fell before they had a chance to find their way out. Then they saw the light coming toward them. It went ahead and came back again as if beckoning them to follow. This they did and soon found themselves in a clearing. The light quickly disappeared.

This story was still being told around St. John's in the late 1950s, but has long since been forgotten.

LOST LIGHT

During the 1930s, a woman at Port Rexton had a weird encounter with a spirit which lead to a death in her family. The story was told by the woman to her grand-daughter who recorded it and offered it to local newspapers to publish. A copy of the short story was in the possession of the late Dr. Bobbie Robertson up to the mid-1980s. Whenever the question of the existence of ghosts came up, Bobbie would retrieve the item from one of her many files at the Newfoundland Historical Offices at the Colonial Building. The item read,

> I would like very much to relate this story to you, which is a factual story that happened to my grandmother. This is how she told it to me.
>
> About twenty years ago she and her husband were living in a settlement on the coast not far from Bonavista and her husband along with her two sons were engaged in the shore fishery. My grandmother said, "It had been my habit when they were out after dark to light a lamp on the beach to guide them back safely, as just 100 yards past our house there were a number of jagged rocks which extended out in the water for a distance of about 300 yards. This night in question I had a very strong feeling of disaster, although it was not unusually stormy. When it came time to put out the lantern to guide them home, I went outside with much misgivings and laid the lantern on the beach.
>
> "I had no sooner returned to the house, and looking out I saw the lantern was out. I ran back to the beach to relight it but in a few seconds it flickered and died. I thought the wick was wet or there was not

enough oil in it. I returned home; put in a new wick and made sure the lantern was filled. I ran back to the beach and again lit the lantern but in a few seconds it once more went out. I never had this problem before.

"I tried and tried for at least half an hour but just couldn't get it to light. I was desperate so I went to a friend's house to ask for help. It took me half an hour to get there and get back with another lantern. My friend came with me.

"However, when we lit the lantern we heard cries of distress on the rocks nearby where my husband's ship had gone aground. Although both my boys managed to get to shore safely, my husband drowned.

"The boys told of how on their return they could not find the light on the beach and had no idea where the rocks were located."

The story became well known to thousands of Newfoundlanders, and for those who already believed in ghosts, it was obvious that the angel of death had called that night for the husband. Skeptics, however, argued it was nothing more than a coincidence.

BURIED ALIVE STORIES

Although part of our Newfoundland folklore claims that many people were buried alive during the various epidemics that often swept communities, very few such stories were given any credibility. The following stories, which are among the exceptions, tell of people being buried alive and the extent of the fear of being buried alive. The first two were reported as news stories and the other printed as a feature ghost story in which the writer claimed the story was true.

GROTESQUE DISCOVERY

Two hunters in the interior of Newfoundland came across a grotesque discovery in 1947 at Mary's Harbour, Labrador. The two, Richard Manuel and Jack Armstrong, reported that when they dug up the coffin of an aged trapper who had been dead and buried for three weeks they made a frightening find. The hands and arm were protruding through the soft wooden coffin top. The man apparently had been buried alive.

There was speculation that he had been in a coma, and when he came out of it, tried desperately to free himself. The coffin had been temporarily buried in three feet of soil by two natives who intended to send it to Cartwright, Labrador.

At the time of the discovery, the Newfoundland Department of Public Health and Welfare explained that in isolated areas it is often not possible to obtain medical death certificates. Unfortunately, they said, it is left for the nearest of kin to notify the department which is what happened in this case.

At the same time this story took place there was a claim that a member of a well-known family at Heart's Content had been buried alive in the family vault. The discovery was made after relatives visited the vault and discovered the coffin overturned and the corpse in a different part of the tomb.

(These incidents were reported in the *Sunday Herald*, 1947).

MOUNT CARMEL CEMETERY BURIAL

The following incident described in a 1940s newspaper feature is claimed to have taken place in the late nineteenth century. In that period a deceased person was taken to the graveyard for burial on a hearse (which was a horse drawn wagon at the time) and only males were allowed to accompany the funeral procession. During one such funeral, two men walking behind the hearse, on its way to Mount Carmel Cemetery, were just a few feet behind the coffin. Their story was told and retold for years afterwards and was known by thousands in St. John's.

One of the men described, "On the way to Mount Carmel, once or twice I thought I heard noises inside the coffin, and once a faint cry. But I dismissed it as pure imagination. Nevertheless, I listened intensely all the way to the cemetery but heard nothing more, except when the coffin was being lowered into the grave." He described that he looked at the faces of the other mourners and there was no visible sign that anyone else had heard anything. The man left the graveyard feeling that his imagination was at work because of his being distraught over his friend's death.

Weeks later he was having a cup of tea with the friend who walked with him in the funeral procession. He told his friend of the spooky feeling he had since the funeral and described what he thought he had heard. His friend exclaimed, "My God! I heard the cries but dismissed them as my imagination . . . . our friend was buried alive."

PARANOIA

In nineteenth century St. John's, the fear of being buried alive haunted many people, especially in the late 1800s when the tales of the Queen of the Dead on Carter's Hill were still fresh in the public mind. (Read *Beyond Belief*, Jack Fitzgerald, 2001.) So spooked was one city merchant that he left detailed instructions in his will regarding how his burial was to be handled. On his death bed he asked each family member to swear that they would honour his wishes. The family were not told what was in the instructions until after he had passed away.

The will reflected the man's terror of being buried alive. He instructed that just before the coffin was to be closed for burial, a doctor would be allowed to examine the body once more to assure that death had taken place. Even with that condition met, the man still did not want to take any chances and he demanded that an open razor be placed in the coffin. If by chance he were to awaken in the coffin, he had the means of ending the horror.

Another man had a light hearted attitude towards death. The most famous eccentric of Newfoundland history, Professor Charles Danielle, requested in his will a special type book to announce to friends his passing. Before his death he prepared the book which featured jokes and the Professor's own opinions regarding his life and death. One of the jokes in the *Death Book* was:

Carbonear man — "I have to move to Harbour Grace next month."

Neighbour — "Don't be so sad, maybe you will die before that time."

He also levelled severe criticism at the people of St. John's for being narrow minded, hypocritical and riddled with jealousy. Unfortunately, no copies of the unique *Death Book* appear to have survived. (For more on Professor Danielle see *Beyond Belief*, Jack Fitzgerald.)

GHOST STORIES

Newfoundland newspapers over the past two centuries have given birth to the many ghastly tales that have become part of our folklore. These stories were presented to entertain and through being published were made known to tens of thousands of people throughout the colony. The following selection presents such stories from newspapers spanning a period from the mid-nineteenth century up to the 1950s.

THE GHOST AT THE GRACE HOSPITAL

In a city with many claims of spooks and spectres, it is inevitable that a hospital would have its share of ghost stories. One of the most interesting of these involved the old Grace Hospital on LeMarchant Road during the 1940s.

A man from Bay Roberts was recovering from an operation when one night, after taking a routine walk through the corridors of the hospital, the man mistakenly returned to the wrong room. He said the lights were dim and he realized, when he saw a woman sitting on a bed in the room, that he had made a mistake.

After apologizing the man turned to leave but the woman pleaded, "Don't go, sit down a minute and talk to me." He recalled that the woman appeared to be very ill. She looked about forty or fifty years old, had blond hair and her face was very white. The man said, "She wore blood red lipstick which gave her a ghostly look."

He felt sorry for the woman but did not wish to stay. "I'll drop by tomorrow and talk to you," he said. "Talk to me now," she pleaded, "I will not be here tomorrow."

The male patient wondered why anyone looking so sick would be going home so soon, "Oh, you're going home?" She nodded and said, "My husband is coming for me tomorrow. He has been in Canada but is flying home by Trans Canada Airlines. I will be alright when he gets here, it won't be the way it was today. I left the hospital today but I came back. I couldn't bear it out there all by myself."

The male patient asked the lady where she had been. She replied, "They took me to a dreadful place. They frightened me. They ought to wait a little longer until somebody comes, but no they couldn't wait. They had to rush me out of here by the back entrance in an awful kind of truck. When we got there it was worse because I hated all their faces and the things they said about me. Nobody there loved me. I couldn't bear it. They shouldn't make you go alone. That's why I ran away and came back for tonight, just until my husband gets here to take care of me."

The male patient was concerned as he left the room. He commented, "Sure, it will be fine when your husband gets here."

Bright and early next morning the nurse came into his room to give him his medication. He asked how the lady in the room next to his was doing. "Oh, she died," answered the nurse.

"That's sad," he said. "Last night she told me her husband was coming back from Canada and she really wanted to see him."

The nurse with an expression of puzzlement said, "You didn't talk to that woman last night. She died at noon yesterday and her body was taken to the morgue in the afternoon. The room has been vacant since then."

THE GHOST OF McMURDO'S LANE

Another ghost story from old St. John's involves McMurdo's Lane. Two men walking up Water Street late one night heard an agonizing moaning coming from McMurdo's Lane. It was one of those nights when fog had slithered in from the Atlantic and was engulfing downtown streets.

The men went into the laneway thinking some poor unfortunate soul had met with an accident and was in need of help. But there was no one there. As they left, they again heard a low moaning sound. This convinced them that someone must be nearby and in trouble. They went up and down the laneway but again could find no sign of anyone nor any explanation for the moaning. Then, appearing out of the fog, the figure of a man began to slowly take form. The two city men stood frozen unable to move. One of them made the sign of the cross saying, "In the name of The Father, The Son and The Holy Ghost." Slowly the figure evaporated.

Over the following years, the men told and retold the story and would claim that at the time of the apparition, they felt they were in the presence of something evil.

McMurdo's Lane, St. John's.

THE HAUNTED CARS

Two well known ghost stories involved haunted cars in old St. John's during the 1940s. The first story tells of a man on Military Road who heard of a car for sale on Southside

Road that was supposed to be haunted. He approached the owner and got what he thought was a bargain. That night he took his ten year old son on a drive to Midstream, now part of Bowring Park. On the way back to town his son glanced in the rear view mirror and suddenly exclaimed, "Look dad, there's a man in the back seat covered in blood!"

The man stopped the car to investigate, and after finding no evidence of anyone being in the back seat, concluded it must have been his son's imagination. Perhaps inspired by the stories being told that day of the haunted car.

Later that night the car owner went to remove some clothing from the car and was startled to see a man sitting in the rear seat. At first he speculated that it was a neighbour playing tricks on him. But when he opened the door he was frightened by what he witnessed. The figure in the rear seat wore a light raglan and soft hat. His head was thrown back, and blood flowed down the pallid face from a wound in the head. The figure looked so real that the owner reached in to touch it. As he did the figure disappeared.

Over subsequent months, others in his family claimed to have seen the same figure. Finally, upset by the mysterious sightings, the owner scrapped the car. When he later encountered the man from whom he had purchased the car from he told him of the ghost in the car. The former owner replied, "Nobody believed me when I told them the car was haunted."

Another story which might have involved the same car was described as not only a ghost story but as an actual news wvent which was reported in a city newspaper in the

1940s. In 1941 a young girl was struck and killed instantly by a Plymouth car driving near Fort Pepperrell. The driver was so distraught that he was unable to drive for months afterwards. Friends persuaded him to take up driving again, and on his first day back in the driver's seat, the car stopped suddenly. He noticed immediately that his watch was showing the same time of day that he had accidentally killed the girl. It was 4:50 p.m. His mind flashed back to that terrible day but he soon regained his composure and felt it was merely a coincidence. Yet, it spooked him enough to sell the car.

The new owner was aware of the car's history but felt the former owner had an active imagination. Then one night while driving along the same boulevard near where the accident had taken place, he noticed through the rear view mirror that there was a girl sitting in the back seat. He asked her how she got there but there was no answer. He stopped the car, got out and opened the back door but the girl was gone. When he told his wife of his experience she demanded that he sell the car. Over the next year the car changed hands seven times and each owner complained of strange haunting experiences.

The car ended up in Bonavista where the new owner tried desperately to sell the vehicle at a bargain price. People who told the accounts swore to its accuracy.

THE DANCE HALL GHOST

This story sent chills up the spines of many a Newfoundlander. It began at Jerry Byrne's tavern and dance hall which was then a few miles outside St. John's on

Topsail Road. Two buddies were going from table to table asking the ladies for a dance; a practice not at all uncommon during the 1940s and 1950s.

One of them showed an interest in a young lady sitting alone in the corner. He sat down at her table, chatted for awhile, then invited her to dance. When their dance finished he thanked her and then went to his friend. He told him that he got the strangest feeling while dancing with the girl; he couldn't put the feeling into words. His friend laughed and to convince him it was only his imagination, he took the girl for a dance. Surprisingly, he too claimed he experienced an eerie feeling while dancing with the stranger.

When the dance was over, the two men offered to drive the young lady home. She accepted telling them that her name was Rose and she lived on Campbell Avenue. It was a chilly night and one of the men placed his coat over the girl's shoulder.

On the way, they chatted and when the car pulled alongside her home, she asked them to wait and went inside. However, a long time passed and Rose did not return. The men decided to leave but first they wanted to get the coat back.

They rang the doorbell and a grey haired old lady answered. When the men said they wanted the coat they had loaned the girl who went into the house the lady replied, "There is no young lady in this house." The men insisted that a girl had entered the house so the lady invited them in to look around. Inside the living room they saw a picture of Rose on the mantlepiece. They pointed to the picture and told the lady, "That's the girl we loaned the coat to." The old lady turned pale, and remarked, "That is my daughter Rose. She died years ago in an accident on Topsail Road."

THE MILITARY ROAD HAUNTING

During the mid 1980s, I talked to a Buddhist monk who lived in St. John's and who had an interest in the history of some of the rivers near St. John's. During the interview he told me of strange happenings which were occurring in a home he owned on Military Road. Several tenants had fled the home convinced that it was haunted. The monk described his effort to cleanse the house of any troubled spirit that might be stranded there. He said several members of his faith joined him, and for several nights, they conducted a service. The service involved turning off all electricity and lighting a room only with candles. The Buddhists then chanted a low humming sound over and over for several nights. He explained the chant had the effect of soothing spirits and a troubled spirit would benefit from their ceremony. Strangely enough, among my collection of ghost stories that had warranted mention in the press over the years and had become known to thousands of Newfoundlanders, I had a story involving the same house.

During the 1920s, Military Road was one of the best residential sections of St. John's. The same house which was now suspected of being haunted in the mid 1980s already had a history of similar claims in the mid 1920s. One newspaper reported, "Strangely enough the apparition apparently chooses the most awkward and embarrassing moment to make its debut, resulting in a regular, and from the renting agent's point of view, annoying stream of tenants.

The strangest reported apparition took place in 1945 during a time when the residence was being renovated. Two contractors were working inside the house on a bitterly cold day; January 3, 1945. The previous day's winter storm had left the city buried in snow. One of the men looked out the window and was astounded to see a small girl, partially clothed, cross the icy road and go up the steps of the house. She knocked on the door and when the men opened it she walked right in. They could not see her face because it was bent over, looking at what seemed to be a small kitten.

The girl went straight to a downstairs dining room. One of the men commented that it was a shame to allow a small child to go out in weather like this. The two resumed their work.

Then they heard the loud sobbing of the child in the dining room which was separated from the kitchen by french doors. They could see the child standing in the room wearing a long cotton dress. They opened the door to see what was bothering her and she suddenly rushed towards them. When they asked what was wrong she looked at them. For the first time they could see her face. It was pale, hallowed eyes and her brunette hair quickly changed to grey. The men fled the house leaving their tools behind. They refused to go back and swore to their employer that there was evil in the house. This was not the first nor the last claim that this house on Military Road was haunted.

Fred Butler who worked longshore claimed that Telegram Alley was haunted. Telegram Alley was the name used to describe the laneway adjoining the old Telegram building on Duckworth Street, and which connected Duckworth Street and Water Street. Fred recalled,

> I was coming home from work one night. It was about 9 p.m. and I had thoughts of the many stories I had heard of the ghost that haunted that lane. I was watching for anything strange. When I got at the concrete steps at the foot of Victoria Street the unexpected happened.
>
> It appeared as if a figure dressed in black suddenly ran in front of me and crossed the street and then ran down Telegram Alley. I ran to the top of the alley and although I was only yards behind the black figure, there was no sign of anyone in the alley. I was spooked by it all. I remembered the many stories of a ghost in that alley but I had never heard any explanation.

The next day Butler told his friend Frank Kane but Kane did not see anything funny in the story. He too was familiar with the ghost story and proceeded to tell Butler the story behind it.

Kane said,

> During the war, a sailor, who had been robbed, was picked up unconscious near that very spot on Duckworth Street and died from his injuries. The killer or killers were never found. That man's spirit is not yet at peace and he will continue to haunt the lane until prayers remove his burden.

Kane and Butler then bowed their heads and prayed for the spirit of the dead sailor.

VOODOO CURSE

Considering Newfoundlanders's long association with the sea, it is inevitable that some of our ghost stories have ties with spooky tales from other countries. The 'Voodoo Curse' from Trinidad is one of these stories. It is said to have taken place in 1945 and like the others told here, became known by tens of thousands of Newfoundlanders during the 1950s.

A St. John's native employed on a Newfoundland ship travelling to Trinidad became romantically involved with a native girl in that country. He made a promise to marry her but had no intention of keeping it. The sailor expected that he would simply sail out of port with his ship when his time came to leave. However, things did not work out that way.

On the day of departure, the man rushed on board and asked his shipmates to hide him. Just as the ship was casting off, a native girl showed up on the wharf demanding to talk to the St. John's sailor. When she was told he was not on board, she shouted that they were lying and said she would cast a voodoo spell on the boat.

Once the vessel was clear of the wharf, the sailor came on deck and joined with the others in laughing at the lady and her voodoo threat. That night however he became a believer. While asleep, he felt invisible hands grab him by the neck and throw him out of his bunk. This happened three times and the man ran to the deck refusing to return to his quarters.

The next day he was given another room but the voodoo curse followed him. He began hearing a voice talking from under his bed. He tried sleeping with the light on in his room but the light would go out on its own. Although he tried replacing the bulb several times, it never lasted more than a few minutes.

His roommate claimed to have seen a pack of cards being shuffled by invisible hands. The crew became terrified by the strange happenings which they blamed on the curse, and by the time they reached New Orleans, demanded that their comrade be asked to leave the ship to break the curse.

The captain arranged for the man to transfer to another ship heading for St. John's. However, while that ship was stopped over in Halifax, the man fell overboard and drowned. His crew mates were convinced that the voodoo curse had finally claimed its victim.

THE SKELETON OF SHOAL BAY

In 1907 a man from Petty Harbour, while digging near his cabin at Shoal Bay, found a human skeleton. Authorities were notified but the remains were never identified. One thing was certain though; the man had been murdered. There was a bullet hole in his skull.

About five years later the cabin owner visited Boston and while there was told an amazing story regarding Shoal Bay. An old Boston fisherman, who claimed to be a descendent of a pirate, related a story handed down in the family about pirate treasure his ancestors left behind in Newfoundland. According to the story, the pirates had buried a treasure estimated to be worth millions of dollars at a place near Petty Harbour known as Shoal Bay. The treasure is said to be buried ten feet northwest of a grave. Many people searched without success for the treasure including the father of Newfoundland — former Premier Joseph R. Smallwood. Even more intriguing is the legend behind the treasure.

In the year 1800, two Petty Harbour fishermen operating out of Shoal Bay (five miles from Petty Harbour) witnessed a very disturbing scene. They watched a pirate ship enter the bay and drop anchor. A boat was lowered into the water and six men with a coffin climbed into it. There were two black men among the six men in the boat. They rowed ashore and the two Newfoundlanders remained hidden nearby wondering what was happening. Several hours later they heard a shot and watched as only five men returned to the pirate ship.

Only later was it learned that the coffin had been filled with gold. The legend claims that the leader of the six men asked for a volunteer to guard the treasure. One of the black crew men volunteered for the position. The captain then raised his musket and fired one shot into the sailor's skull. The body was then buried in a grave near the treasure. The pirates held the superstitious belief that the dead man would forever guard the treasure. The pirates left and never returned. Perhaps intervention of the law may have disrupted their plans. But the story was preserved and handed down from generation to generation. Strangely, the Bostonians' legend seemed to give some credibility to the legend that lingers in Petty Harbour.

Over subsequent years, there were many reports of sightings of a large, dark man leaning on a rock near the treasure site.

THE HAND FROM THE BOG

During the 1930s a man from St. John's moved his family to Markland (south of Whitborne) in hopes of being able to provide for his family. It was the period of a six-cent-per-day dole. At Markland he was employed on a Government make-work project clearing land at forty dollars an acre. However, he later claimed he encountered a real spirit.

One evening, just as he was leaving the field, he heard a low sounding moan coming from the bog area he had cleared earlier that day. He slowly walked towards the sound. The sun was setting and darkness was spreading over the land. Suddenly he saw what appeared to be an arm sticking out of the bog. The fingers were moving. The St. John's man rushed to the site thinking someone was trapped in the bog, but when he got there the arm had disappeared. He grabbed a long stick and began probing the bog area but found nothing.

At first he thought someone had sunk in the bog but then realized he had been working in that area all day alone. All the way home he puzzled over the encounter and finally concluded it must have been his imagination. By the time he got home he had decided he would not mention the incident to anyone.

Three weeks passed and the man had just about forgotten the event. Yet once again he heard moaning and looked in time to see a hand waving from the bog. At this point he was about twenty feet away from the hand and could see it in great detail. Between the fingers was heavy caked bog. The hand was deadly white and as he approached, the hand slipped beneath the soil. He was now confident it was not his imagination. He took his spade and began digging. He dug down several feet but could not find a trace of anything strange.

That evening he told his wife the uncanny story and she was horrified. The next day the couple went to Whitbourne and told the story to an old inhabitant of the area. He told them that about thirty years before, a man named Patrick McGrath from Trinity Bay disappeared somewhere along the Markland Road. The man said, "In those days the bog lands were more dangerous and more swampy than they are today. It was believed he went off the road and was lost in the bog."

The following morning, the St. John's man placed a wooden cross on the spot where he had seen the hand. The cross remained there for years and the mystery hand was never seen again.

BELL ISLAND'S BABY GHOST

The story of the baby ghost of Bell Island was well known in Newfoundland during the 1940s. According to the tale, a young unmarried girl gave birth to a baby boy and then murdered him to hide the secret of her pregnancy. Using a pillow, she smothered the baby, then wrapped the body in heavy brown paper and burned it in the fireplace.

The girl was unable to live with the secret and became physically and mentally ill. She complained of hearing the soft cries of a baby wherever she went. Shortly after she was sent to the Waterford Hospital in St. John's.

Her family had remained in the house and, soon after the girl's departure, began telling friends that they often heard the sound of a crying child at night. Before the daughter died, she told her parents her secret. They sold the house and moved to St. John's. Over the next several years, the house changed hands many times and every tenant claimed to have experienced the same encounter with the ghost baby.

While many were convinced the house was truly haunted, others suggested the crying sound of a baby was actually the wind blowing into the crevices on the side of the house. They claimed that the girl and others who became aware of the ghost story accepted it without question. The house remained vacant for years afterwards.

THE PHANTOM LADY OF MOUNT CARMEL CEMETERY

A story often told in parts of St. John's during the 1930s and 1940s, especially on cold, stormy winter nights, described the ghost of a lady dressed in black who haunted the road near Mount Carmel Cemetery on The Boulevard.

The first of the many sightings reported over the years took place during 1907 and Johnny 'Pop' Kelly swore it was true. Pop was walking up The Boulevard late one night when he suddenly became aware of someone a few feet ahead of him and walking in the same direction. When the light of the moon broke through the passing clouds he was amazed to see the figure of a woman gliding along in front of him. Overcome by curiosity, he increased his pace and spoke to the lady saying, "Good night, ma'am." There was no reply.

He then suspected the lady may have been a disguised friend playing a prank on him. He approached the lady to get a closer look and asked, "How are you tonight ma'am?" She turned and looked straight into his face. Her face was pale, her eyes were sad but she did not speak. Pop said he suddenly got an eerie feeling. At the gate of Mount Carmel Cemetery she turned and walked in, and as his eyes followed her, she disappeared.

Pop went to his friend's house near King's Bridge and told his story. He told it many times after that, and as the years past, others also claimed to have seen the ghost they called, 'The Phantom Lady of Mount Carmel.'

VOICE FROM THE GRAVE

Three fishermen who spent several nights on Little Bell Island during the 1930s told of a strange encounter experienced while they camped there. The three men had been jigging cod in the area and decided to stay out on the island for a few days.

On the first night one of the men named Walt Fillier said he was awakened by the sound of someone calling his name. Thinking that one of his friends was calling him, he sat up and looked around the campsite but saw that his friends were both sleeping. He listened carefully for a few minutes and finally convinced himself it had been his imagination.

Four times during the night the voice called his name, "Walt." Fillier knew that apart from a few stray sheep brought over that summer by farmers, he and his two friends were absolutely alone. He became anxious and decided to wake his friends Kevin and Edward. He described his experiences and the trio tried to find some explanation. Finally they all agreed that they were being visited by a spirit.

Edward told Walt that if the spirit called his name again he should make the sign of the cross and say, "In the name of God leave me alone." The men drifted back into a sleep. Near 4:00 a.m. Walt was awakened again by the spirit's call. This time he felt there was a presence close to him but he could not see anyone. He recalled that the voice was whispering in his ear.

He sat up and did as his friends suggested. He blessed himself and said "In the name of God leave me alone," whereupon he heard the most horrifying supernatural screech he had ever heard. The noise even woke Kevin and Edward. The men were so frightened that they decided then and there to row back to Bell Island. The trio never again set foot on Little Bell Island.

THE BLUEBERRY FIELD GHOST

The following story is said to have taken place near Beaver Pond during the 1930s. Mrs. Bessie Connolly of Southside Road took her two sons berry picking near Beaver Pond. After filling their crocks they decided to boil-up. The fire was going well and they were enjoying their outing when suddenly they heard a cry for help. All three heard the cry and looked towards the area where the sound had originated. They began walking the path towards Beaver Pond when they heard the cry again.

They ran to the pond and while standing near the water heard a scream ending with a gurgling sound. It seemed to be coming directly from in front of them. However when they looked closer, they saw that nobody was in the water and the water was calm. Mrs. Connolly grabbed her son's arms and rushed back to the campsite. She quickly put out the fire, gathered up their belongings and headed down Blackhead Road towards home.

They told their story to neighbours who had lived in the area much longer than the Connollys. The neighbours, however, were not surprised. They had heard the same story many times over the years. They claimed the stories started after a man drowned in Beaver Pond. All agreed the cries were from a lost soul.

THE CENTRAL FIRE HALL GHOST

For decades St. John's was abound with ghastly tales from the old Central Fire Hall. If there was indeed a lost soul haunting the building it must have left when the old fire hall was torn down and replaced with the present one. At least we no longer hear haunting tales of the Central Fire Hall in St. John's.

The late Bill Tibbo, who lived on McFarlane Street during the late 1940s, swore that there was a spirit haunting the building. Tibbo, a fireman who worked in the building, said that strange things happened there not only at night but often during the middle of the day.

There were the frequent tapping sounds coming from the upstairs area. Although the men searched the area for an explanation none could be found. Tibbo said it could not be explained by the wind because it occurred sometimes even on days when there was no wind. At night a low moaning sound engulfed the whole building. Some firemen said you could not escape it no matter what room you were in.

Central Fire Hall in St. John's

Another manifestation of the haunting was that sometimes when the men sat around the table to have lunch a strange presence would be felt in the room. It was always accompanied by a very cold feeling which lasted for several minutes and then left. Doors could be heard opening and closing upstairs when there was nobody there. Tibbo said his most terrifying memory of the spirit presence was when he was having a cup of tea alone in the lunch room. He said it felt like someone was watching him but there was no one around. Then a chair at the table began to shake and actually moved on its own. He called to his fellow workers who quickly responded but the manifestation had ended. Tibbo said after that he sprinkled holy water around the building and placed a pair of rosary beads on each floor of the building. Tibbo swore the hauntings stopped after that.

The fire hall was built on the site of the old Government House where Sir Francis Pickmore froze to death. Pickmore had petitioned the Colonial Office in London for a new and warmer building. He was told to rent or find a boarding house in the city for that winter. However, fire destroyed the city and Pickmore was unable to find a suitable place. He froze to death in the house on February 24, 1818. When he died his body was placed in a puncheon of rum and sent accross the Atlantic to London for burial.

For decades it was believed that Pickmore's spirit haunted the site of the old Government House. Tibbo believed Pickmore's spirit never left and had taken up residence in the old fire hall. One last fact, according to Tibbo, was that it was 6:00 p.m. on February 24 that he witnessed the moving chair. This was not only the anniversary date but the exact time of the death of Governor Pickmore.

For years after leaving the fire hall, Tibbo told his stories to the patrons of the old Esquire Lounge, and, he always held the conviction that he had been in the presence of the old Governor's ghost.

SPIRIT WORLD

Sometimes people unwittingly arouse the resentment of the spirit world by intruding into places once treasured by a departed spirit. Such may have been the case at Carbonear during the 1920s.

A Mr. Dawe purchased land adjacent to his property upon which to build a house for his family. Mr. Dawe succeeded in erecting the whole frame for his house in one day. When the daylight faded into darkness, he called it a day and went home for supper and a good night's rest. At sunrise the next morning, Dawe took his tools and headed for the work site expecting to make even better progress than the previous day. He was astounded to find that the entire structure was lying on the ground. Dawe was mystified. He asked himself, "Was there a defect in my scaffolding? Perhaps the soil was soft beneath the structure." Not one to waste time, Dawe set out again to put the frame back in place. By nightfall he had finished the task.

The following morning, he returned to the site hoping to continue the project. Dawe was again astounded to see that the frame was scattered around the ground, broken and splintered. It was a total mystery; that is until an old neighbour told him the sad history of the property.

Dawe learned from the neighbour that four people had lost their lives in a house fire that destroyed the family residence which occupied the property more than fifty years before. The house was occupied by a man, wife and two teenage sons. According to the old-timers tale:

> During a windy, cold wintery night, fire broke out in the house. The man tried to rescue his wife and children, but without success. His wife had rushed to the attic bedroom to rescue the two boys and all three became trapped. Help arrived too late to stop the fire or save the three trapped family members.
>
> At the funeral he told friends that he would never allow a house to be built on the site again. He was so distraught that several days later he hanged himself. No townsperson ever showed an interest in the property because they believed it was haunted.

The old-timer then told Dawe that the destruction of the house frame was no mystery. It was the dead man's spirit making good on his promise.

THE SPECTRE OF PORT-AUX-GAUL

Every community in Newfoundland has ghost stories or stories of strange encounters. A most intriguing story comes from the old community of Port-aux-Gaul. During the 1890s two men from the community set out on a hunting trip. When darkness began to settle in they realized they were a long way from home. Being experienced woodsmen they set up camp near a beach.

No sooner had they settled down for the night when they were disturbed by the sound of footsteps approaching their camp site. The two sat up in time to see a man in uniform whom they believed to be a naval captain. They jumped to their feet and saluted the officer. The military man took no notice of the men and stared straight ahead as though they did not exist. He walked straight to the beach.

The men followed close behind. They saw a boat waiting and wondered as the officer went on board. No sooner had the officer boarded the vessel, when it vanished into thin air. Over the years the two often told the story to friends, relatives and anyone willing to listen. There was no doubt in their minds that they had encountered a being from the spirit world.

A DEADLY WARNING AT BLANC-SABLON

Newfoundland folklore is full of tales of the supernatural and many include stories of tokens who warn of pending disaster. James Benoit, who lived at Blanc-Sablon around 1900, told of a horrifying incident which sent chills up his spine.

While eating supper one evening, a stranger rushed into Benoit's home and pleaded with him to come and help. The stranger was visibly upset and Benoit anticipated something terrible had happened. He told Benoit that there had been a wreck nearby and the ship was sinking. He said the need for help was urgent otherwise the crew would be lost. When they arrived at the seashore, Benoit looked up and down the coast but could not see any signs of a ship. He turned to question the stranger but he had vanished. Dumfounded and scared, Benoit rushed home. For two days Benoit was troubled by what had happened. He heard many stories of tokens and portents but had never experienced one. As a matter of fact, he thought of them as old-wives tales. But now he wondered.

Three days after the incident, a severe wind and rain storm struck the area. In the early morning daylight, Benoit could see a ship in trouble a few hundred yards off-shore. Benoit was among the men from the community who set out to aid the troubled vessel and rescue its crew. The rescue party managed to save eight of the crewmen and recovered the bodies of three more who had drowned. James Benoit was astounded when he recognized one of the drowned seamen as being the man who had come to visit him days before with a plea for help.

MESSAGE FROM THE GRAVE IN RENEWS

Ambrose Cahill, a native of Cappahayden, had many intriguing stories of the Southern Shore to tell me. One involved a troubled spirit and a message to the living from the grave.

The incident took place aboard a vessel which had gone aground near Renews Harbour. Some men from Cappahayden were on board salvaging the cargo when one of them noticed a stranger walking on the deck. He made no mention of the encounter at the time because he didn't want, ". . . to be chided" by his friends.

While his friends worked below-deck, he began explor-ing the upper area of the ship. Several times he saw the stranger and when he approached him, the stranger would vanish. Frightened by the encounter, the Cappahayden man rushed below deck to tell the others. After listening to the incredible story, the others laughed, suggesting, "The stranger could make no claim on this ship's cargo."

The man asked the others to go with him and check out the story. He argued with sincerity that, "this was no mortal man. It was a spirit who appeared to be on a mission." The small group of fishermen made their way through the ship and to the cabin where the spectre was last seen. They were amazed to find a picture still wet on the floor of the room. Amazed because there was no sign of water anywhere in the cabin. The picture showed a woman with the inscription on back, "To Walter from Catherine with love." Also written was the address of the woman.

The men took the picture ashore and mailed it to Catherine along with a note explaining how they found it. The fishermen were sure that the picture had, ". . . come from the bosom of her lover in the deep who wanted it known that he had been true to the end."

GHOST SKIPPER OF RENEWS

During the 1920s, two fishermen became strong adversaries. Their confrontations lasted a lifetime and continued even beyond the grave. The story, said to have been told by the son of one of the men, began in the parish hall at Renews. According to the storyteller his father had won the hand of the girl that the other man had hoped to marry.

The story claims that there was a terrible fight at the wedding between the groom and the ex-boyfriend and he, ". . . cursed the union and prayed that no good would come of it." From that day on the two men never got along together and when they met there was always a heated argument. They even argued at church and would pass each other on the road without uttering a word.

According to the story, the man who had cursed the wedding years before, later got in trouble at sea when his engine gave out and he was drifting toward nearby rocks. The other man who was close enough to help refused to provide assistance. Fortunately, another boat in the area came to the aid of the man in trouble in time to prevent his boat from crashing upon the rocks. When the same man died of a heart attack some years later the other refused to attend the funeral. He went as far as to predict that, if the rulers of hell would allow him, his enemy would return to haunt him. The thought was prophetic.

Within months, the living fisherman became convinced that he was being haunted by the dead man. His boats mysteriously broke their moorings and his home was destroyed by fire. As a result, his savings were used up in an effort to replace his losses. In desperation, the man sold off everything and purchased a schooner for the Labrador fishery.

At the end of his first voyage he was feeling his luck had changed. He had a successful season and the trip had been without any major problems. Just as he began thinking the curse of years before had been broken, a terrible storm struck. The high winds were forcing the schooner toward the rocky coast and certain tragedy. The fisherman began cursing and blaming the turn of luck on the ghost of his old enemy.

His son later told friends that just as they were giving up all hope of survival, a strange thing happened. He remembered his father standing at the wheel trying desperately to keep control of the vessel. His father later told him that he felt another hand placed over his on the wheel and a voice beside him say, "Don't worry, I'll get you out of this. I've made you suffer enough," his son explained. It was the voice of his old enemy. From that moment on things improved. The fisherman was able to control the vessel although he swore that it was not his strength that brought her around but the guiding hand of his former enemy at the wheel.

When the schooner pulled up to the wharf in Renews the fisherman said, "If you can hear me show yourself so that I will know for sure that it is you." The son swore that at that moment the dead man appeared long enough to reply, "I'm leaving for good now." For years after, both the fisherman and his son told the story and swore to its veracity.

RETURNS FROM A WATERY GRAVE

Several veterans of WWII living in St. John's were amazed in 1947 when they saw a ship that had been sunk in 1945 tied up at a wharf in St. John's Harbour. Navy veterans Harry Carew and Bill Bennett had been in London and boarded the *British Empire Starlight* before it set sail for Russia. Less than a month later they learned that the *BES* had been sunk and sent to the bottom during a Nazi air raid on Murmansk Harbour.

They wondered if the ship they knew as the *British Empire Starlight* was the ship then in port at St. John's. The two veterans took a closer look and saw the ship was named the *Murmansk* and was flying the Russian flag. It had stopped over at St. John's on its way with a cargo to New York.

Harry Carew told an *Evening Telegram* reporter about the ship and the reporter soon clarified the mystery of the *BES*. The captain confirmed to him that the *Murmansk* was indeed the former *BES*. He explained that after it was sunk by the Germans, it lay on the bottom of Murmansk Harbour for two years. A Russian shipping company purchased the ship and had it refloated. They installed a new engine and completely renovated the vessel. The *BES* was built at Hong Kong in 1941. It was the first Russian ship to arrive in St. John's after the war.

ORANGE CLOUD PHENOMENON

In 1995, while driving with two friends across the Witless Bay Line we witnessed a strange phenomena. It was a warm August night with clear skies except for the occasional passing cloud. I was accompanied by two friends: Ambrose Cahill and Evelyn Geary. About half way across the Line driving towards Bay Bulls, one of the clouds attracted our attention and I quickly brought my car to a stop. I had never seen anything like it before. We got out of the car and gazed into the eastern sky towards St. John's at one particular large cloud that was filled with orange light. The light was contained totally within the cloud and it was pulsating. It would go from dim to bright orange then dim over and over again.

A few minutes later another car pulled in and a man and woman got out and joined us. They too were amazed.

None of us had any idea of what we were witnessing. While we watched a series of jagged like lightning bolts moved from one end of the cloud to the other; never exiting the cloud. We all had witnessed lightning storms before both in and outside Newfoundland but never anything even similar to this.

The flashing lights were not as bright as lightning and they remained a constant orange colour alternating from bright to dim. There was no accompanying sound. The cloud appeared not to be moving and we marvelled at the phenomena for about half an hour. We were convinced that thousands of others in the area must have also witnessed the spectacle. I turned on my car radio to get the news, but there was no mention of this event. We then went to a friend's house in Bay Bulls to see if they had watched the cloud. We were really surprised to find that no one we spoke to that night at Bay Bulls or in St. John's had witnessed or heard of the sighting.

The next day I listened to several people on *Bill Rowe's Open Line Show* describing strange lights they had seen in the sky the night before. The calls came from Bonavista and Conception Bay. A news item later in the day reported that the Gander weather office had been questioned about the lights and said it was likely an electrical storm. If that was the case it was indeed a rare phenomena because the entire storm took place inside one cloud.

THE CANDLELIGHT SPIRITS OF QUIDI VIDI

Some years ago, while sharing book-signing duties with Newfoundland's great story-teller Al Clouston, I mentioned that in my book *Up The Pond* I had written about a double tragedy at Quidi Vidi in 1906. Al told me the story was well-known to him because one of the victims was a close relative. He then went on to relate a bizarre incident preceding the tragedy.

The Clouston family lived in a house on Forest Road overlooking Quidi Vidi Lake. One night just before bedtime, Mrs. Clouston looked out the window towards the swimming pool at Quidi Vidi (the sandy beach east of the present boathouse). It was late at night and the area was usually deserted. However, this time something strange was happening.

She saw what appeared to be a burning candle and as she watched, another, then another appeared so that in a short time a semi-circle of candle-light lit the night at the swimming pool. She watched the spectacle until the lights suddenly disappeared. The next day she mentioned it to the rest of the family but nobody could offer a satisfactory explanation for the mystery candle lights.

A week later on August 4, a few days after the St. John's Regatta, Herbert Bancroft and Ted Clouston decided to go for a swim at the Quidi Vidi Pool. A new swimming aid called 'Flying-wings' had been introduced to the market and Herbert and Ted each had purchased the new item. They couldn't wait to try them out at Quidi Vidi.

The boys were having a great time when Ted Clouston slipped out of his float and disappeared beneath the water. When he didn't resurface, Herbert tried desperately to save him but both boys drowned. When given the sad news of the deaths, Mrs. Clouston felt she had the explanation for the mystery candles.

This was not the first incident involving mysterious candles at Quidi Vidi Lake. Mike Murphy, author of *Pathways to Yesterday*, often told a story of a candle-carrying spirit boat on Quidi Vidi Lake. In telling the story, he would credit the famous Johnny Burke, the Bard of Prescott Street, as his source. Burke had rowed in several regattas and for years was an active member of the Regatta Committee. In recalling old-time regattas, he would often tell of the mystery boat on Quidi Vidi Lake a week before the 1884 St. John's Regatta. According to Murphy, a fellow named Crane from Wickford Street (now Livingstone Street) had been trouting one night at Quidi Vidi Lake. When darkness began to set in, he packed his belongings and got ready to leave the lake. He had not seen any boats on the pond for nearly an hour and was startled to notice the sudden appearance of a boat on the pond near the northeast shore.

This was no ordinary race boat. It remained stationery but the occupants were holding candles. As he walked up the bank to a main path, he would occasionally glance back. By the time he reached the path and looked back again, the boat had disappeared. All the way home he wondered what he had witnessed.

A week later, during the Young Fishermen's Race, the Torbay crew rowing in the Terra Nova got into trouble after taking on water when turning the buoys. Just passed Coaker's River, about forty yards from shore, the Terra Nova went down. Three young rowers lost their lives that day.

Crane, after hearing of the tragedy and that it had occurred in the area where he had seen the candle lights, remained convinced for the rest of his life that he had witnessed an omen of the 1884 Regatta tragedy.

JUSTICE

Newfoundland's rich historic past is abundant with criminal tales as chilling and mysterious as those found anywhere. This section features an intriguing collection of such stories. Included are such bizarre and brutal stories as the account of a father slaying his son and that of a son murdering his father. There is also the heartbreaking story of the disappearance and murder of a pregnant young Newfoundland girl in Boston.

Other stories reveal criminal secrets; like the story of the Knights of Columbus Fire of 1942 which offers a solution to that mystery. Another story exposes a skeleton in the closet of the 13th President of the United States which has a Newfoundland connection. Some stories arouse suspicion — like the story of the disappearance of a valuable collection of Newfoundland coins and stamps from the old Newfoundland Museum. A bizarre story unfolds in the account of an unclaimed fortune and the drowning death of an heir to that fortune in St. John's Harbour.

Several strange discoveries in St. John's add to the long list of unsolved Newfoundland mysteries. For example, the discovery of ten skeletons beneath a St. John's street or the skeleton of a giant man from beneath a building at Her Majesty's Penitentiary in St. John's. Other tales give an insight into the limited methods of police and justice officials in pre-confederation days. When a riot broke out at Her Majesty's Penitentiary, guards had to resort to setting off the fire-alarm box on Forest Road to summon help in controlling the uprising. With topics ranging from grave robbing to multiple murders, I expect this section will make compelling reading.

Ronald Watson, a Newfoundlander who migrated to Vermont, made news headlines across the United States in 1946 after committing the most gruesome murder the State of Vermont had witnessed in more than forty years. After his execution, the Canadian magazine, *Greater Detective Cases,* ran a feature story with the front page headline, 'The Riddle of the Slain Cabbie.'

Watson had worked with his father as a fishermen in Newfoundland. He first moved to St. John's and worked longshore and fishing to make a living. When friends told him of the American-Newfoundland Farm Agreement he enrolled. The Agreement provided Newfoundlanders with airfare and shelter to move to New England to work on the farms. One of his few belongings was a fishing knife.

One night he had been drinking and socializing at a bar several miles from the farm where he worked. Henry Teelon was the unfortunate taxi driver who picked up Watson that night. Teelon tried to engage in conversation but Watson was nervous and reluctant. Teelon did not return home that night. Early the next morning the police found his corpse hung over a barbed wire fence and covered in blood.

The police officer noted that there were three gaping holes in the back of Watson's coat as well as two visible knife wounds in the victim's neck. Teelon had been badly beaten and butchered. His forehead over the left eye had been completely crushed.

The investigation lasted several weeks. Vermont police followed up on numerous leads and finally tracked Watson down after finding his name in the victim's 'call book.'

Watson, was the last name written in the book. The Newfoundlander was arrested at the home of his fianceé Joyce Green. He quickly confessed to the killing explaining that his motive was robbery. Watson told police he wanted to buy an engagement ring for Joyce and robbed the cabbie to get the money. Henry Teelon had been murdered for his day's take which totalled $106.

Watson explained that he viciously attacked Teelon because he could not get up enough nerve to take the money. He wanted to be sure Teelon was dead first so he stabbed him repeatedly. The murder weapon was his fishermen's knife which he had brought with him from St. John's.

The trial was a short one. It took place in the Supreme Court of Vermont and captured headlines all over the United States. Ronald Watson was found guilty of murder and sentenced to be executed by the electric chair. He became the first person to be electrocuted in Vermont since 1906.

MURDERED AT BOSTON

In less than ten years, another Newfoundlander was the centre of a murder case in the United States which attracted numerous newspaper headlines. This case however was very different from that of Watson's. The Newfoundlander in this situation was the murder victim. The killer may have gotten away if it were not for a tip that came from St. John's.

Mary Anne Fahey gave up a job in a downtown St. John's store and moved to the United States on May 1,

1928. She had just turned twenty-six years of age. Mary Anne was reluctant to move at first but did so after being encouraged by her sister and brother-in-law who were living in Lynn, Massachusetts, a city just twenty miles south of Boston. They persuaded Mary Anne that if she came to the U.S. they would help her find work. She had no way of knowing that acceptance of the invitation would eventually lead to her death.

Mary Anne had no trouble finding a job in the only shoe store in Lynn. It did not take long for the industrious young lady to work her way up from saleslady to forelady. Through her place of employment she came into contact with a handsome young Italian-American named Amaelo Di Seto and fell in love. Di Seto failed to tell Mary Anne that he was engaged and soon to be married. When she discovered she was pregnant, she tried to share the news with him. Mary Anne penned a short note and had a friend deliver it to Di Seto. The note read, "Come see me dear, I have something important to tell you." Several days passed and her Italian lover was ignoring all her pleas to meet with her. Finally she threatened to tell his parents that she was pregnant. Amaelo gave in and arranged to meet Mary Anne at Market Square in Boston.

When the two met, Di Seto showed no signs of being angry. In fact he proposed that they go to New York and get married right away. She agreed, but Di Seto had other plans for Mary Anne. She did not return home nor contact her sister. Nor did she call in at work. Her disappearance was reported to the police and a search was initiated.

Three days later her body was recovered from Boston Harbour. Police concluded that the girl had been depressed after finding out she was pregnant and had committed suicide. That would have been the end of the story if it had not been for a report in the Newfoundland papers that Mary Anne Fahey had committed suicide in Boston. A young man in St. John's who had dated Mary Anne before she moved to the U.S. had kept in touch with her by mail. Not long before she had written him with the, ". . . good news, that she was pregnant and looking forward to getting married." How could someone so happy kill herself? The man penned a letter to the Chief of Police in Boston and told him of his opinion on Mary Anne's death. He suggested that the police find a gentleman by the name of Amaelo Di Seto, ". . . Mary Anne told me she was going to marry him."

The police followed up on the tip and learned that Di Seto had indeed married another girl days after Mary Anne Fahey had disappeared. The case was reopened and Amaelo Di Seto was arrested and tried for murder. He was found guilty after a short trial and sentenced to death in the electric chair. That sentence was carried out.

HEIR TO FORTUNE DROWNS IN HARBOUR

While Newfoundlanders were preparing to become Canada's tenth province, a St. John's man disappeared. Police were informed and friends and relatives were questioned in an effort to find out what may have happened to him. Thirty days after he was reported missing, the man was found floating face down in St. John's Harbour.

Although the death was determined as an accidental drowning, circumstances in the man's life causes one to wonder if foul play had not taken place. The man, Frank

Viquers, was one of fourteen possible heirs to the multi-million dollar Garrett Estate in Pennsylvania. Eleven of those heirs were Newfoundlanders.

The Garrett Estate represented the fortune left by Walter Garrett and his wife who had no children. Walter made his millions from tobacco and snuff production and distribution. During World War II, the administrator of the Garrett Estate invested $15,000,000 in Victory Bonds at three and a half per cent interest. By 1946 the estate had grown to $33,000,000.

When word of the unclaimed wealth made international news, 20,000 people claimed to be heirs to the money. However, legal advisers employed by the estate reduced that number to fourteen legitimate claimants; eleven of these in Newfoundland.

Frank Viquers had been aware of the estate for more than ten years. He quietly pieced together a family history to establish his claim to the Garrett Estate. His efforts brought him into contact with Mrs. Henry Nelson of San Diego, California, who became one of the fourteen acknowledged claimants. Together they shared information.

No doubt the eleven Newfoundlanders who had a chance of sharing in the fortune were relatives of Viquers in this province. Mr. Viquers had traced his family tree to 1607. In that year Edward and Elizabeth Garrett, of Abbott Skerwell of Devonshire, England, were the founders of the Garrett wealth. Their daughter, Anne Garrett, came to Newfoundland and settled in a cottage overlooking Quidi Vidi Lake. The rest of the family moved to Philadelphia. Anne Garrett married in to the Ruby family, who in turn married into the Viquers family. In 1946 these families were the Garrett heirs living in Newfoundland. Frank had been making the case on their behalf.

Walter Garrett, who belonged to the Philadelphia side of the family, passed away in 1895, leaving his fortune to his wife who was of German descent. She in turn, died at age eighty-four with no heirs. The multi-million dollar fortune reverted to the Garrett side of the family.

Frank Viquers had lawyers in St. John's and Philadelphia advocating on behalf of the Newfoundland claimants to the estate. In 1947 the estate was being administered by the Orphan's Court in Philadelphia. However, before the matter was concluded, Viquers drowned in St. John's Harbour. There was certainly no suggestions of foul play at the time. The family accepted the explanation that Frank, who wore very thick glasses because of vision problems, likely had fallen over the Long John Bridge in the west end of St. John's while crossing to visit a brother on the Southside.

UNEXPLAINED AT HER MAJESTY'S PENITENTIARY

Workmen on a project inside Her Majesty's Penitentiary during the mid 1940s made a gruesome discovery while digging beneath the old broom factory inside the prison yard. Just a few feet under ground they found a hunched-up skeleton of a man. At that time authorities believed only three men had been buried inside the penitentiary. However, the graves of all three had been disturbed so often during various excavations that eventually they were placed inside a common coffin and reburied. The mystery then was, "Who was the man buried beneath the broom factory?"

The story caused a commotion for a short period. Very little information was forthcoming from authorities and there was much speculation among the public. The *Sunday Herald* reported that the skeleton was a giant over seven feet tall. It reported, "He had huge bones, and the skull was abnormally large, with only one tooth missing out of the jaw." The article noted the man had been dead for, ". . . a good number of years." It also speculated that, "Some old-timers seem to think that the man was one of the crew who came over on the viking ship which landed some years ago in Newtown, Trinity Bay, and one member of the crew, a huge Viking over seven feet tall, came to St. John's, but mysteriously disappeared and was never heard of again."

After researching the story I developed my own theory as to the identity of the mystery skeleton. First, there was a fourth person buried inside the prison yard, who after almost three quarters of a century, had been totally forgotten by 1946. That man was Patrick Geehan who was executed during July 1872 after being convicted of murdering his wife and brother-in-law at Harbour Grace. (Full story in *Ten Steps To The Gallows* by Jack Fitzgerald.)

Although Geehan was said to be a tall man, he certainly was not seven feet tall. No doubt the man's height was exaggerated. It seems likely to me that this mysterious 'Giant Skeleton' of Her Majesty's Penitentiary was the remains of the unfortunate Patrick Geehan.

Of the five people executed inside the walls of HMP, Geehan remains the only person whose body has not been removed from its burial place. Three others, Frank Canning, Wo Fen Game and William Parnell, were

removed from their burial place and reinterred at the
Roman Catholic Holy Sepulchre Cemetery on Topsail
Road, St. John's.

NEWFOUNDLAND MURDER AND MYSTERIES

THE 13TH AMERICAN PRESIDENT

The thirteenth President of the United States, Millard
Fillimore, had a skeleton in the closet with a
Newfoundland connection. His great-great-grandfather
John Fillimore once served as a pirate out of Placentia with
Captain John Phillips, a notorious pirate of the eighteenth
century.

Phillips came to Newfoundland to work. He settled in
Placentia and for awhile trained in ship building. Unhappy
with the long hours, low wages and slave-like working conditions, Phillips turned to piracy. He recruited a crew from
Newfoundland and St. Pierre, and in a short time had a
fleet of thirty-three ships. Among the pirate crews was
John Fillimore. Phillips sometimes forced prisoners to serve
with him and it is likely that Fillimore was among those.

Several of those who had been captured and forced to
serve formulated a plot to seize control of the pirate moth-
er-ship. Lead by Andrew Harding, the men attacked the
pirate crew by using carpenter tools. The cries for help
alarmed Captain Phillips who rushed to the deck to see
what was happening.

Phillips was hit with a caulking hammer and then
attacked with an axe. After he was killed, his hand was cut
off and placed on the yard arm of the ship. His head was

then cut off and pickled. The mutineers locked the others below deck and took them to Boston where they were turned over to authorities. Phillips' head was placed on public display in the city of Boston.

The captured men were placed on trial for piracy; a crime which demanded execution on the gallows. Fillimore was acquitted and settled in New England where he lived for the remainder of his life.

OUR STOLEN HISTORY

A treasure of Newfoundland coins and stamps from the nineteenth century vanished during the Commission of Government years and have never been found. These were the property of the Newfoundland Museum and very much a part of Newfoundland's heritage. What happened to them? Nobody really knows. They may have been destroyed in a fire, lost or possibly may still be gathering dust in some government office building. It is most likely however that they were stolen.

Curator Leo English, of the revived Newfoundland Museum in 1952, made great efforts to track down the treasure. However it was to no avail. On the surface it seems like an easy question to resolve. That is until one considers that the entire contents of the Newfoundland Museum were scattered in storage areas in and near St. John's. It is very likely that this is a mystery that will never be solved. Yet, it is a story worth recording.

The collection of items that ended up in the Newfoundland Museum began with a private effort by some wealthy citizens of St. John's prior to 1817. In that year a display called "The Cabinet of Curiosities" containing Newfoundland artifacts was open for public viewing at the Free Mason's Tavern on Solomon's Lane. Decades later, James P. Howley and Alexander Murray lead the effort to persuade the Newfoundland Government to take over the collection. In 1886, the Government purchased the entire collection for fifty pounds sterling. Space for the new museum was provided on the top floor of the old Water Street Post Office. In 1907 the Museum was moved to the old Gosling Memorial Building on Duckworth Street.

Old Railway Station, Fort William, St. John's (now occupied by Fairmont Newfoundland) c. 1890.

Unfortunately one of the first acts of the Commission of Government in 1934 was to close down the Museum. Due to lack of storage space, the collection was spread throughout the city and sometimes in unusual places.

Curator Leo English told the *Evening Telegram* that all zoological exhibits were stored at the fisheries experimental station at Bay Bulls, where they were later destroyed in a fire. The minerals and the still aquarium went to Memorial University. The fossils were sent to the old Sanatorium Laundry; their labels were lost in transit so that they became useless. At the sanatorium they were regarded as a heap of rocks and at one time a construction firm asked for permission to embody them in a concrete structure.

Old Railway Yard, St. John's c. 1880. (Site of present Fairmont Newfoundland.)

Mr. English said that other relics were put in cold storage at the railway station in St. John's but later moved to the Sanatorium Laundry. Some were lost, some were stolen and others were damaged in transit. Mr. English was unable to determine the destination of the safe with the coins and stamps at the time they were moved. Most of the coins and stamps in the collection were from the nineteenth century. In addition to their cash value, these items had great significance to Newfoundland's heritage.

Before the items were removed from the Museum, an inventory was taken which included mention of a safe containing the collection of rare stamps and coins. In the early 1950s, when the Museum was reopened, the coins and stamps could not be found. Even the safe had disappeared.

Old Post Office, Water Street, St. John's.

Despite an intensive effort to locate them, the items were never recovered. They may very well be gathering dust in some out-of-the way room in one of our old St. John's buildings or a major theft may have taken place!

FIRST ARREST OF A SEAGULL

The first and only time in Newfoundland's justice history in which a sea gull was arrested and locked up in the city jail took place in 1948. Police were called to Barnes Road where a man grasping the leg of a sea gull was lying on the street in a pool of blood.

It was apparent to police that the man had been attacked by the gull which was trying to break free. Although the bird was picking at the man's face, he held tightly to it and refused to set it free. The frustrated police officer gave up trying to reason with the drunk and arrested the man and the gull with him.

Before the man was taken into court next morning, the gull was taken from him and kept in a cell. The man was found guilty of being drunk in public and fined. However, he refused to leave the court house without his gull. The police unlocked the cell and the man was allowed to take the bird.

Not only was this the only time in Newfoundland that a man and gull were arrested but also the first time that a man and gull were cell mates for the night.

THE COURT HOUSE PROPERTY

A famous building in old St. John's was called the 'Market House.' It was a three story building that opened on July 6, 1859, with John Boone of Flower Hill (now Springdale Street) as keeper.

The building included the market on the first floor, a post office, jail and telegraph office on the second floor, and the courts on the third floor. In designing the jails the architect set out to exclude all the light that he possibly could. Old records describe the jail as a, ". . . dingy, dark place."

Market House Square, Water Street, St. John's c. 1890.

The Market House had an entrance from the side as the courthouse has today. The stairways resembled a medieval dungeon and were called 'Shea's Hall.' The area now occupied by the courthouse steps was called Market House Hill. Daily auctions took place at the Market House after which people sat around on barrels to discuss the issues of the day. Patrons shared a common pewter mug to avail of the clean water available from a well in the base-ment. It is claimed that lawyers learned more law through their barrel-debates than they did in court.

MURDER IN MONTREAL

During the summer of 1910, William Shute, a Newfoundlander working longshore in Montreal, attracted newspaper headlines across Quebec after killing fellow worker William Mercer. However, as details of the killing became known, sympathy grew for the Newfoundlander, and by the time his trial was over, the public was supporting Shute.

Evidence presented at the trial showed that Mercer had harassed and tormented Shute for months leading up to the confrontation that led to Mercer's death. Many of his remarks were aimed at insulting Shute's mother. Meanwhile, Shute was shown to be a quiet gentle person and non-aggressive. Witnesses expressed the opinion that they could not understand how Shute took the insults for so long without losing his temper.

Shute did reach a breaking point. One day when the two were unloading a ship in port, Mercer heaped insult after insult on Shute. He then made lewd comments regarding Shute's mother. Shute moved towards Mercer demanding an apology but Mercer continued to jeer Shute. A struggle followed which ended with a bruised and battered William Shute, and with William Mercer lying dead on the wharf.

The jury didn not take long to acquit the Newfoundlander. Although Shute had thrown the first punch, the jury felt that he was provoked and had no choice but to defend his mother's character. Shute had been charged with murder and if convicted, would have been certainly executed.

GATHERING OF KILLERS

A rare event in Newfoundland criminal history took place in 1947 at Gander. A plane carrying thirty-five convicted murderers made a stop-over at the airport town. The plane was closely guarded by armed guards. The killers were responsible for more murders in the United States than had been committed in Newfoundland during its previous 450 year history. The plane was at Gander most of the day and during the time the passengers were not permitted to leave the plane.

Prior to World War II, the United States sent dangerous criminals back to their country of origin. However, it was not practical to do this during the war years and the number of prisoners to be transferred steadily grew to thirty-five. Most of these were being sent to Italy and Greece, and many of them were involved with the American Mafia.

THE TEN SKELETONS

Workmen digging up a foundation on Job Street made an alarming discovery during the summer of 1922. Ten skeletons were found buried on the property. Newspaper reports stated that one skeleton had a completely black head. It was never determined how long they had been dead. Old-timers were unable to remember having heard anything about bodies being buried in the area. Some of the speculation at the time and for years afterwards claimed that all ten were men and there were signs they had met a violent death after enduring torture. It was claimed that each had the right arm and left leg broken and two of them had their hands broken off.

A newspaper in St. John's in 1947 reported that a complete investigation was never carried out into the discovery. The question was raised at that time that it might have been a mass murder. News of the discovery caused a commotion around St. John's, but in time, interest dissipated and the ten remains were never identified.

The *Sunday Herald* asked, "What crime was committed in the dark past of Newfoundland's history?" It remains a mystery as to how these ten men were murdered and successfully hidden, so that it was not until years later that their tortured skeletons were discovered. It is rather odd that with the ten skeletons only one pair of shoes were discovered, while over their bodies hummed a shoe factory turning out thousands of pairs a year.

MURDERED HIS DAD

The five minute summary given by the defence in the murder trial of seventeen year old Basil Young in 1945 is perhaps the shortest summation in Newfoundland's criminal history. Not only was the summary brief, but no witnesses other than the accused were called by the defence. Even stranger was that when the accused was cross-examined by the crown prosecutor, he admitted to the killing and testified that he knew the consequences of his actions. At first glance one might wonder why the defence lawyer even showed up in court. Yet he scored a victory of sorts. At the time hanging was the penalty for a person convicted of capital murder, but Young escaped the gallows. Although it sounds very much like a simple cold-blooded killing, the facts tend to stir sympathy for the convicted man. Defence lawyer Jimmy Higgins calculated correctly that he had no chance of an acquittal. His battle was against the gallows for Basil Young. Higgins placed his faith in the belief that once the court heard the details of the tragic relationship between Basil and his father, it would not apply capital punishment.

Basil Young had been the victim of a cruel father who had both physically and mentally abused him. The depths of the man's cruelty was evident in the fact that after his wife died, he threw his family out of the house. He kept Basil, who was five years old at the time, but forced three older brothers and a sister to leave. Perhaps it would have been kinder had he also forced Basil to leave.

Basil was kept from school and was forced to work for his father. The man beat the child with his fists, kicked him and on one occasion during hay making stabbed him with a pitchfork. At age sixteen Basil was illiterate. He was overjoyed to get work on the American Base at Harmon Field in Stephenville. Unfortunately, the job did not last long and Basil had to return home.

When he tried to enter his family home, his father refused to allow him to stay so Basil went to the home of Joseph Young. On June 1, his father allowed him to stay for the night but threw him out the next day. Basil went to the home of neighbour William Aucoin. In the afternoon he sent young Cecilia Aucoin to Mary Young's store to buy him a .22 cartridge. He said he wanted to put it on his bike as an oil cap. But the mentally tortured Basil Young had murder on his mind.

That evening he found himself sleeping on the floor at his cousin's, Laurence Young. The brutality and abuse at the hands of his father was playing heavily on his mind. Unable to sleep, he got up at 2:30 a.m., dressed and removed his gun from the wall and walked to his father's house. The door was unlocked and Basil entered. He asked his father, who was awake, for a lamp. His father answered, "I don't know if I will let you have one at this hour."

Basil then asked if he could stay the night but his father shouted, "I don't think I will let you stay." Mindful of his father's cruel streak, Basil claimed he became frightened when his father moved to get up out of bed. He took the shell from his pocket and put it in the gun. He then fired at his father. Mr. Young fell back onto the bed and the blankets fell to his waist. Blood poured from the body and soaked the bed.

Basil Young calmly put the blankets over his father's body, took a flashlight and a house key from the dresser and went out. He locked the front door after him. Following that Basil acted as though nothing had happened. He returned to his cousins, placed the gun back on its rack, then lay down on the floor and went to sleep. The next morning he invited Laurence Young to go with him to his father's house. He failed to mention that he had shot his father. While Laurence examined Basil's bicycle which was stored in a bedroom, Basil was in his father's room.

He calmly took a pair of pants from his father's room and went back to his own room to change. After telling Laurence he was going to mass, he left the house. But he did not go to church. He went to the home of Mary Marsh where he spent the night. On Monday he returned to his father's home and returned the clothing he had taken. Afterwards he gave the house key to his uncle Ben.

Before the day was over the police were at the Young home and Basil was arrested by Ranger Terry and Lt. Glendenning. The prosecutor was Hon. H. R. Winter. Defence lawyer Higgins called only one witness — the accused.

Under cross-examination by Winter, Young admitted that he arose that Sunday morning with the intention of killing his father and he replied that he did. When asked if he was aware of the legal consequences of his act, he again replied in the affirmative.

Jimmy Higgins was very brief but to the point in his summary to the jury. The theme of his address was that Basil Young was only a boy with no education whatsoever and had not had an easy life with his father. He finished his comments in just five minutes. The prosecutor took eighteen minutes to complete his summation. Trial judge, Justice Sir Brian Dunfield, explained to the jury the legal requirements to prove murder.

The jury retired but returned with their verdict in eighteen minutes. It was no surprise to the filled courtroom when the jury chairman announced its 'guilty' verdict. Basil Young, dressed in a checkered woolen windbreaker and a pair of khaki pants, remained expressionless as the Judge pronounced his sentence that Young be detained in prison. Young had escaped the gallows.

Members of the jury included: George Brown, Arthur Garland, Thomas Bailey, Frank Munn, James Ridgley, John Badcock, Ernest Snelgrove, Michael Mulcahy, George Phillips, George Stone, Clarence Reid and Noah Blake.

SHORTEST TRIAL AND THE RAREST SENTENCE

The shortest murder trial, including appeal, sentencing and execution in Newfoundland criminal history took place in just three days during October, 1794. The event also included a penalty rarely used in Newfoundland. In handing down sentence to the two men who had been found guilty of murder, the judge sentenced both to hang with the added indignity of dissection.

This strange episode in Newfoundland's criminal history began when Captain Arthur Morris of the HMS *Boston* obtained permission from the Governor of Newfoundland to seek volunteers from among St. John's residents to fill vacancies in his crew. The effort was unsuccessful and the captain invoked his right to press (conscript) men into Her Majesty's Service. A ship's press gang searched every public house in the city and brought fifteen men to the captain. Eight of these provided the captain with good excuses as to why they could not serve and were released. The remaining seven were ordered to serve.

Among these were two Irishmen who asked for permission to go ashore to gather some personal belongings. Lt. Richard Laury with a group of four sailors escorted the two to shore. In the area now occupied by Steers Cove a gang attacked the escort, killed Laury and set the two Irishmen free.

In a matter of hours the British had the ring leaders of the gang in custody. The two men were tried on Wednesday, October 29, had their appeal heard on October 30, and were executed on October 31.

The two men were dressed in white turbans made of two to three yards of linen and escorted from the waterfront to the gallows at the Barrens, near Fort Townshend. The executioner wore a long black cape, face mask and a wig made of black sheep's wool. After execution, the bodies of the two men were turned over to local surgeons for dissection.

ATTACKER BECAME A VICTIM

A rather strange incident in Newfoundland justice took place near Cape Ray in 1942 when an armed attacker became his own victim. When twenty-seven-year-old Jeremiah Wall, a Cape Ray fisherman, confronted the young Lucy Osmond, he was armed with a gun. When the girl resisted his advances, he struck her with the gun and then threatened her. The feisty-spirited girl fought back viciously, and in the scuffle, the attacker accidentally shot himself in the leg three inches above the knee.

A doctor was called from Port-aux-Basques, and after bandaging and treating Mr. Wall, arranged for him to be taken to the hospital in Stephenville. The man was escorted by a Newfoundland Ranger. What would have been the fate of the woman had she not fought back will never be known. But Wall never attacked anyone else. He was never arrested and never saw the inside of a jail. Wall passed away at 6:00 a.m. after the attack from his self inflicted wound.

CAMERAS

The use of photography in crime fighting is so routine today it is hard to imagine that its effectiveness was once questioned. The St. John's *Evening Mercury* of January, 1882 printed the following news item:

PHOTOGRAPHY OF CRIMINALS — Does the photographing of criminals really lead to their identification? An answer to this skeptical query is at once afforded by the Berlin police, who not only keep a criminal album, but note its uses. Last year, it seems, no less than 130 persons, arrested for crime in the capital and suburbs, were identified by the album, whose names were entirely unknown, or who had given false ones. This number—representing nearly one-third of the total arrested for serious crimes—could not have been identified, say the police, without the album. In Berlin, they wisely do not portray every convict, but simply habitual criminals and those against whom heavy charges have been brought.

FINGERPRINTING

Criminal history was made in St. John's on August 6, 1934, when the first court conviction based on fingerprint evidence was recorded in our court system. The case involved the trial of George Williams for breaking and entering the home of Mrs. Edwin Murray of St. John's. Fingerprints left on a window used to gain entry to the Murray house were introduced as evidence in the case. Based solely on this fingerprint evidence, Murray was found guilty.

Not only was this the first time in Newfoundland and Canada that fingerprint evidence alone had won a conviction, it was only the third such case in the British Empire.

MANUSSING

Manussing was a crime in nineteenth century Newfoundland. Captain H. Lewis of the schooner *Mary* returned from the ice fields on April 19, 1862, and summoned eleven of his crew to court for 'manussing' (refusing to work) and forcing him to abandon his voyage. The men were convicted and Magistrate T. Peters of Harbour Grace sentenced three of them to twenty-eight days imprisonment and the other eight to fourteen days.

BUSTED OUT OF A PORTUGUESE PRISON

Martin Murphy brooded for several years over his father's imprisonment in a Portuguese prison and then set out to do something about it. The younger Murphy set out from St. John's in the early 1930s for Portugal with the intentions to break his dad out of prison. Murphy Sr. had already spent five years in one of the most notorious of Portugal's prisons.

Martin was not alone. He had the support and help of the crew members of a Newfoundland fishing vessel which happened to be in the Portuguese port at the time. In an article written by L.J. Delahunty in 1946 and published in the *Sunday Herald*, the story was first told to Newfoundlanders.

The article stated:

> The story goes back sometime to a night when Newfoundland sailors mixed it in a free for all in a Portuguese café. Murphy, senior, attacked a Portuguese to whom he administered a lusty beating. Called to court he had to face a hostile room using a poor interpreter and no one was very surprised when the trial was shelved.

So far as the court seemed concerned, Mr. Murphy, an Irishman who had raised his family in Newfoundland could rot in jail. There could be no shortening of his term, since he had not been sentenced. But five years later, Marty, the eldest son reached Portugal and sought to find his father.

In his quest he was finally successful and by bribing some guards, he located the prison where his father was. Making his presence known, he succeeded in smuggling his father a piece of paper (delivered by a bribed guard) saying that if his father could manage to slip his guards, and drop from the wall of the prison at a certain time on a certain night, help would be on hand.

We can very well imagine the risk this involved on both sides. It meant curtains for those who engineered the escape; and for Patrick Murphy it was the end of his hopes of ever again seeing his loved ones of his native land! But it was his only hope, and probably his last, so he agreed heartily.

Marty, meanwhile, made known his plans to his friends. They volunteered to a man to make the attempt. On the appointed night Patrick Murphy dropped from the prison wall into the arms of his countrymen who succeeded in smuggling him aboard their ship. Despite a thorough search carried out daily aboard ship he was brought back safely to Newfoundland.

How did he effect the escape? Well, the facts are that on that night when his guard entered Murphy's cell, Murphy doused him with a shovelful of ashes, backed up by a punch to the chin, which was all that was needed to put him out cold.

KIDNAPPED

The late Don Morris, journalist, columnist and archivist, was a great collector of Newfoundland oddities. One of his stories told of a remarkable encounter between white set-tlers and the Beothuck natives of Newfoundland during the early nineteenth century.

The story told of a white man being kidnapped by the Beothucks. According to the tale, some fishermen involved in constructing a schooner were being annoyed by snowballs being hurled at them from a wooded area nearby. One of the men went to investigate the source of the snowball attack.

The others paid little attention and went on with their work. After some time had passed without hearing from their friend nor having to fend off snowballs, the men expressed concern over their comrade. They stopped working and began a search of the nearby area shouting the man's name over and over. However, there was no response. They discovered many footprints in the snow but no sign of any living person. The fishermen concluded their friend had been kidnapped.

Twelve months later, one of the men, while rowing along by the shore, was startled when from out of the woods ran a man who jumped into the water and swam towards the boat. He was dressed in Beothuck clothing and covered with red ochre in Beothuck style. The fisher-men recognized him as their kidnapped friend.

Close behind the man, a small band of Beothucks gath-ered and shouted in their native tongue. Among them was a native woman holding a baby in her arms. She waded into the water beckoning for the man to return. The man told his friend to move away as fast as possible. As they rowed into the distance the man told his amazing story to his friend. He said that when he went into the woods to see who was throwing the snow balls, he was attacked by the natives and taken into the interior.

During his months of captivity, he was treated well and married a Beothuck woman. The story does not tell whether or not the baby the native woman carried belonged to the white-man.

BODY SNATCHING

During the eighteenth and nineteenth centuries in Newfoundland, the taking of a body from a grave was not considered theft. Newfoundland was governed by British law and that law did not consider such an act as a theft. The reason, ". . . no property being recognized in the remains of deceased relations after they have been buried."

During the eighteenth and nineteenth centuries, grave-robbing was common in Britain, Ireland and Scotland, but not in Newfoundland. Graves were robbed most often to sell bodies for scientific purposes to universities which trained doctors. However, sometimes parts of a dead body were stolen for less lofty purposes. Occasionally, people extracted teeth from the dead to use as false teeth. There is some oral history in Newfoundland of teeth being extracted for this purpose but no record of any person ever being charged with such an offence; possibly due to the law as it existed during that period.

Scotland had the same law, but there was a distinction between the two. In British territories, under no circumstances could the taking of a dead body be considered a theft. In Scotland however, an indictment for theft was held good for the abstraction of a corpse before burial. This was an important distinction at a time when stealing above the value of five shillings (one dollar) was punishable with death.

In regards to the subject of stealing dead bodies, British Supreme Court Justice T. Stephen raised the question, "Can skeleton and anatomical preparation of parts of dead bodies or which formerly formed parts of bodies when living, be stolen? Teeth, for instance, intended to be used as false teeth." As silly as it seems, this question remained unsettled in British justice for more than a hundred years.

GALLOWS ODDITIES

At the time of Francis Canning's execution in 1899, the *Evening Telegram* claimed that all executions in the colony up to and including that date were carried out during bad weather; mostly, heavy rain and thunder and lightning storms. No doubt this led to a great deal of superstition amongst the population. Some even believed that electrical storms were heavenly signs that an innocent person had been executed. (Canning had been hanged at Her Majesty's Penitentiary for the murder of his bar-maid Mary Nugent.)

The newspaper commentary covered executions back to 1806, although there were many prior to that. It referred to the 1806 hanging of a man named Farrell for the murder of his wife. Heavy winds and torrential rains pelted the city on the day Farrell was executed.

The story stated:

> Farrell worked as a pilot at St. John's Harbour. In those
> days boxes were placed under Signal Hill, somewhat
> above where now stands the bathing house and in line
> with the railway track. (Public swimming took place in
> the harbour near the battery and a public bathing
> house was built nearby. The railway station at the time
> was on the site now occupied by The Fairmont
> Newfoundland and the tracks went down across
> Plymouth Road to the waterfront.)
>
> The duty of this water pilot (Farrell) was to remain
> out in his boat all night, going to the Southern Shore
> in search of ships. Upon the night of the murder, sen-
> tries were on duty as usual in their boxes and Farrell
> was noticed by them not to go out this particular time
> until daylight.
>
> A squad of soldiers saw him resume his duties at
> an unusual time and knowing what had occurred at
> his house arrested him and the boat's crew. He was
> found guilty of murder and condemned to be hanged.

At that time there was a gallows standing on what is
now the eastern gate of the Roman Catholic Basilica and
the Mercy Convent. Other gallows in St. John's were
Gibbet Hill on Signal Hill; the waterfront where the Royal
Trust Building now stands and the lower eastern corner of
the Anglican Cathedral grounds at Church Hill. When the
Church expanded their cemetery adjacent to the
Cathedral, the gallows was moved to Gallows Hill. (Now
Bate's Hill. At the time a river flowed down the hill to the
Harbour).

The next tragedy involved the multiple slaying of a
woman and her family near Rawlin's Cross by a man

named Robin Barry. This crime was detected by a military captain walking in his garden near Rawlin's Cross. He saw Barry running and covered with blood. The captain drew his sword and arrested Barry. Barry was placed in the city prison to await trial. However, he escaped the gallows by strangling himself with his braces.

Horse and sleds near the site of the present day Fairmont Newfoundland. St. Thomas' School is in the background.
c. 1890's

Soldier's Meadow and St. John's Harbour c. 1880.

Old Railway Station, St. John's c. 1890s.

During 1898-1899 when labourers were digging up the street at Rawlin's Cross, they recovered the body of Robin Barry. It was believed that Barry was deprived a proper burial because of his suicide and was laid to rest on his family property at Rawlin's Cross.

There is a final oddity of our execution history that is intriguing. The *Evening Telegram*, while referring to the hangings of the eighteenth and nineteenth centuries noted, "When we look back at these records, if there be any circumstances which should occupy the minds of our fellow-countrymen, it is this, namely: that almost every crime of this nature committed in this country may be traced to those of foreign birth. It is a matter of congratulation that in Newfoundland there have been less crimes of the above kind committed than in any other of Her Majesty's possessions."

MYSTERY OF THE GIBBET

The foul deeds of Paddy Malone and Peter Downing of Harbour Grace are told in my book *The Hangman is Never Late*. The two were sentenced to be hanged, but Downey who played the most active role in the killings had the added punishment of gibbeting added to his sentence.

After he was hanged in St. John's, his body was placed aboard the stagecoach going to Portugal Cove. From their he was placed on a packet going to Harbour Grace where the gibbeting took place. However, the body was mysteriously removed at night and left on the steps of a witness in the trial.

More than fifty years later the *Evening Telegram* commented on the mystery. It stated:

The body was cut down (in 1833) and it has never been known to this day how it was done, as the lower portion of the gibbet was of iron, deeply sunk in the rock. It was the iron that was cut. It was then brought to the door of Dr. Stirling's residence, and placed upright against it, with a letter in the hand. The servant opened the door and the body fell in and upon the paper was found this legend.

Doctor, doctor try your skill
For I am Downey from Gibbet Hill.

Dr. Stirling was a witness in the double murder trial.

DESTROYING GIBBET HILL

Gibbet Hill near Cabot Tower remains as a reminder today of early justice in Newfoundland when the gallows played a prominent role in law enforcement. However, by the late 1930s, the hill was in the process of being destroyed when St. John's City Council intervened and stopped the destruction. By the time this action was taken, almost half the hill had been removed by city contractors using it as a stone quarry to build and repair city streets.

Amazingly, Newfoundland historian Judge D.W. Prowse as early as 1895 had called for a stop to the contractor's destruction of Gibbet Hill. It was already established as a stone quarry at that time and action to preserve the site was not taken until nearly fifty years later. The *Evening Telegram* in 1937 while calling for a stop to the destruction noted, "The rock at the foot of the hill is of the same formation as that at the higher level. If quarrying operations were carried on in the Battery, the work could be so conducted that as the material was removed, a route for a road could be cut out at the same time."

During the eighteenth and nineteenth centuries, Gibbet Hill was also known as the Crow's Nest and formed part of Wallace's Battery.*

* Reference to the Crow's Nest and Wallace Battery contained in research paper by Mrs. Harold Ayre published in the *Evening Telegram*, August 1937.

THE 'BOBBY'

It has been a well known fact that an English policeman is known as a 'Bobby.' The origin of the strange name for the English police began at the time when Sir Robert Peel, a noted British aristocrat, served as Secretary of Home Affairs in the late 1820s. Prior to being appointed to cabinet, he served as Under-Secretary of War and as Chief Secretary for Ireland. Sir Robert had the notable reputation throughout British Empire as being, ". . . hard as nails."

Peel was very disturbed by the crime wave sweeping England at the time. He declared to the public that he would stop the trend and he persuaded Parliament to pass the Metropolitan Police Act. To enforce the law he imported scores of rough and tough Irish constables.

Peel's admirers nicknamed him 'Bobby.' The new constables were known as 'Bobby's men.' Over time the term was abbreviated, and the familiar Bobby has been applied to the British police force ever since.

IT WAS THE LAW

In 1884 a law was made in Newfoundland that any dog other than a Collie or a small dog would be considered a wolf and should be destroyed. A hundred years earlier, Newfoundland families had an average of six dogs per family. These were used as work dogs and were later replaced by horses. In 1780 Governor Edwards issued a proclamation that only one dog per family was allowed. The reasoning behind this was aimed at developing a sheep industry in Newfoundland. Dogs were destroying sheep herds at the time. Between 1825 and 1835 Governor Cochrane introduced a law demanding that horses be used instead of dogs in road construction. Eventually the horse replaced the dog as a work-animal in Newfoundland.

STRANGEST TAX

Newfoundlanders were once required to pay a special tax to cover the costs of transporting a gang of Irish convicts out of the country. This episode in Newfoundland's justice history took place in 1789 when Mark Milbanke served as Governor. He penned the following letter to the magistrates throughout Newfoundland:

> Gentlemen,
> A committee of the merchants and traders and inhabitants of this place (St. John's) having been appointed to take into consideration the dangerous state of this island from the many idle persons now in it, particularly a number of nearly 100 who were some time since landed at Petty Harbour and Bay Bulls, and

who are at present under the care of a guard at St. John's upon a supposition of there being Irish convicts; and also to consider of the best means of raising a sufficient sum of money to send the said convicts out of the country, and the said committee having come to a resolution and giving it as their opinion, that St. John's should bear one half of the burden of the expenses, and the rest of the island who are equally interested in getting rid of such banditti, the other half, and that the proper mode of raising it would be by assessment the following manner . . .

The tax was determined as follows: every merchant-owned or operated ship had to pay ten shillings each. All fishing shallops with four men to pay four shillings; skiffs two shillings and six pence; and every citizen three shillings. Governor Milbanke ordered the magistrates to arrest any of the Irish convicts in their communities and send them to St. John's. Sufficient money was collected to send the convicts out of the country. They were transported on the ship *Elizabeth* under Captain Robert Coysh. Old bedding was gathered from the military forts and placed on the ship for the convict's use. The Governor's written order to the captain was, "You are to make the best of your way with them to Spithead, Ireland, where you are to wait the command of His Majesty's ministers."

A BIG SWINDLE

A meeting of 200 people at the British Hall in St. John's in 1911 and the sinking of the *Titanic* in 1914 were major parts of the fantastic story of the $1,000,000 unclaimed

Churchill Fortune in England that has intrigued Newfoundlanders for almost one hundred years. Influenced by the stories, several Newfoundland families held hope that one day they would find the proof needed to claim the fortune. Recently acquired information however, has dashed such hopes forever. A potential heir to the alleged fortune went to England in 1990 armed with a copy of the Churchill will, and after some research in London, confirmed that the estate had been settled on November 23, 1867.

How then did such an incredible story take root and inspire hundreds of claims on both sides of the Atlantic? What convinced some to mortgage their homes to pursue the claim? And why did it take 120 years for the truth to be revealed?

The answers may be found in the evolving story of the Churchill Estate. My first knowledge of the story came from my uncle, Ed Martin whose ancestors (on the Boland side of his family) formed part of the group who felt they had a claim to the fortune. His knowledge of the claim came from his parents, but pursuit of the unclaimed estate had ended with the alleged loss of legal records in the sinking of the *Titanic*. From the information he gave me, I set out to see if there was an actual untold amazing Newfoundland story to be written. After reviewing hundreds of old records, I finally came across the story of an allegedly unclaimed Churchill Estate and the details obtained from my uncle were confirmed in these dusty old archive records. In 1986 I included these findings in my book *Amazing Newfoundland Stories*. The story revived interest in the fortune in Newfoundland, New York and Boston.

I learned that in 1911 a public meeting was held in St. John's of descendants of Samuel Churchill, an Englishman who came to Newfoundland in the eighteenth century and over his lifetime accumulated a fortune in Newfoundland and England. When Samuel died his fortune was left to his son Nicholas who was killed by pirates shortly after receiving the inheritance. It then was passed on to his (Nicholas) daughter with the stipulation that if she died it would go to his (Samuel) two sisters in Newfoundland. Lady Churchill (daughter of Nicholas) ignored her father's wishes and upon her death left everything to her own children. The family in Newfoundland contested the will but passed away without it being settled. At least that is the story that evolved in Newfoundland.

An intriguing aspect of the story was that the Churchill family in England included the family of Sir Winston Churchill who had appointed a relative, the Duke of Marlborough, to handle their claim. The Duke sought to determine the number of possible heirs to the claim and sent a lawyer to St. John's and New York to seek out the answer. According to the story told to Newfoundlanders, on one of the lawyer's trips he carried with him historical documents that would help settle the estate. His journey was never completed as he was an unfortunate passenger on the *Titanic*.

A notable part of the story is that each time it was reported in the media over the last hundred years, the value of the fortune got larger and larger. It went from a moderate estate to a multi-million dollar estate then to a hundred million dollar estate that included large tracts of valuable property in St. John's and England.

Since the publishing of my book, *Amazing Newfoundland Stories*, there has been sporadic public interest in the item. I have received calls from people across Canada and in the United States relating to the story. However, it was only recently that I was acquainted with facts that show the story was either a swindle or a remarkable example of legal incompetency.

During the summer of 2001, Philip Babcock of Atlanta, Georgia, while visiting relatives at Bay Roberts, was reading my book *Amazing Newfoundland Stories* when he came across the story of unclaimed fortunes. The story caught his attention because it included the name of Elizabeth Churchill, one of his ancestors, whose grave he had visited that week at Ochre Pit Cove.

Mr. Babcock had researched hundreds of Newfoundland stories in the past and this was one mystery he was determined to solve. He described his reaction that night, "I could hardly sleep a wink after reading all this. My mind reeled as I considered how I could find out more and where to go, who to ask; should the estate still exist what happens now that Newfoundland is no longer a colony, etc.?"

Over the following months, he tracked down relatives in Newfoundland and on the mainland. His effort brought him in contact with Robert Halfyard (another descendent of Samuel Churchill). Robert Halfyard from St. Catharine's, Ontario, had compiled a book called *The Halfyard Family Register* which traced his family to Richard Halfyard (1744-1815) and Elizabeth Churchill (1752-1828).

Mr. Babcock was kind enough to call me from Atlanta during the Christmas season of 2001 and share his findings with me. The true story differed from the one that had survived in Newfoundland. Mr. Babcock had learned that Samuel Churchill died about 1772 leaving three children; Nicholas, who was married with two children; and two daughters, Elizabeth and Clarimond. Elizabeth had married Richard Halfyard of Ochre Pit Cove and Clarimond married Maurice Boland. According to Mr. Babcock, Samuel Churchill disinherited his daughter Clarimond because she had married a Roman Catholic.

One reason why so many people readily accepted lawyers' claims that the estate had remained unclaimed was that the children and grandchildren of Elizabeth and Clarimond kept the story alive. Mr. Babcock, remembered his aunts claiming that there was a family inheritance in England and two lawyers had gone there to determine its veracity. He added that there were rumours that another branch of the family had prospered after the lawyers returned and it was believed they had gotten some of the money. This rumour convinced many of the Bolands and Halfyards in Newfoundland that an unclaimed fortune did exist.

By 1911 there were many ancestors of Maurice and Elizabeth (daughter of Samuel) Boland living in St. John's. Not only did an oral history of the fortune exist in Newfoundland, but in 1911 the story began receiving international attention. On August 2, 1911, according to Babcock, a New York newspaper published a story of the unclaimed Churchill Estate. The newspaper gave a plausible explanation of why the estate had never been settled. It claimed that when Samuel died he left his fortune to his son Nicholas with the condition that upon Nicholas's death his (Samuel's) two sisters in Newfoundland should get the remaining estate.

The newspaper noted that Nicholas had been captured and killed by pirates and that his will was never found. His two sisters in Newfoundland could not provide proof that they were legitimate heirs and so, the Newfoundland government took the property owned by Nicholas Churchill in Newfoundland and auctioned it. This claim prompted two granddaughter's of Clarimond, living in Boston, to sue the Newfoundland Government for eighty-five million dollars. Other variations of the will were put forward in the press but all with the same conclusion that an unclaimed fortune existed.

The story grew bigger and received international attention which brought forward claimants to the estate from New York, Brooklyn, Vancouver, England and Newfoundland. Philip Babcock observed that, "Given the vast size of the purported estate and the fact that a number of lawyers were involved, it is doubtful that anyone with even the remotest connection to the two Churchill sisters wanted to be left out of this potential windfall."

Mr. Babstock's efforts to find out more about the remarkable story ended when he contacted Richard Halfyard in Ontario. Halfyard had obtained a copy of the will of Nicholas which confirmed that he had left his estate to his children Elizabeth and Nicholas Jr. There was a provision in the will that should the children not survive to age twenty-one the estate would go to his (Nicholas's) sisters in Newfoundland. Both children lived long beyond the age of twenty-one. Elizabeth survived her brother and died at the age of 84 on April 17, 1867, in the County of Devon. Neither Elizabeth nor Nicholas Jr. had married. Elizabeth bequeathed the entire estate to her cousin and the will was settled on November 23, 1867.

Mr. Babstock noted several reasons that may explain how the story of an unclaimed fortune survived for so many years. First, there was information available by 1990 that may not have been available to researchers in 1911 and 1912. Nineteenth century documents related to the estate were not all placed in the public archives or public domain by 1912. There was the variety of interpretations of the will which encouraged the belief that the estate had remained unclaimed.

Philip Babcock enjoyed his search and was fascinated to find its ending. However, he said the story did generate a lot of money. He was referring to the maybe tens of thousands of dollars collected in legal fees by lawyers representing the heirs. Was it all a deliberate swindle; legal incompetence; or maybe just unavailable information? Whatever the answer, it remains one of Newfoundland's incredible stories.

CHIEF JUSTICE — HUMBLE START

George Summers was castigated at a City Council meeting during March 1938 and he didn't take the attack lying down. He hired one of the most brilliant lawyers in St. John's and met Council head on in Council Chambers.

The incident began during the weekly meeting of City Council when Councillor Meaney accused Summers of exploiting workers by underpaying them and by failing to meet the conditions of a snow clearing contract with the city.

St. John's had been paralyzed after a major snow fall early in March. Summers offered to provide snow clearing on Duckworth Street, New Gower Street and Water Street for $1,100. City Council appealed to the Commission of Government to pay the snow clearing contract claiming it was for $1,200. The Commission agreed to pay half the cost, and the city ended up with a commitment of $600 rather than $550.

290-296 Water Street, St. John's, between Beck's Cove and Malone's Lane c.1910.

When Summers offered to hire an extra forty men to shovel snow for an additional hundred dollars the city agreed. It was during the depression, and Council to its credit, never missed a chance to hire labourers when financial resources were available. However, when it came time to pay Mr. Summers, Councillor Meaney stood up in Council and demanded that $200 be withheld because he had evidence Summers had not fulfilled the conditions of the contract.

He then went on to castigate Summers. Meaney accused the contractor of exploiting the workers and not paying them according to the commitments in the contract with the city. He said he had evidence that Summers had paid the shovelers working on Duckworth and New Gower Streets twenty-five cents per hour while those on the Water Street detail received only fourteen cents per hour. Councillor Meaney added that he had gotten many complaints that Water Street had not been properly cleared. Having maligned the character of Mr. Summers, Councillor Meaney said he would gladly apologize if it turned out he had been wrong.

George Summers was outraged. He asked and was given permission to appear before Council with his lawyer. It was customary in those days for citizens to be allowed to appeal directly to Council and to appear in person to plead their case. Summers, however, sat quietly while his lawyer presented his case.

The lawyer held a copy of the contract in his hand and asked Council to read it carefully. It was not a lengthy document. The lawyer noted the contract mentioned that workers on the Duckworth Street and New Gower Street detail be paid twenty-five cents per hour. But it did not mention any figure for those working on Water Street. He said these workers were made aware before they started that their pay would be fourteen cents per hour. In respect to the uncompleted work on Water Street, the lawyer pointed out that there had been a snow fall after the contract was signed and George Summers was not libel for this. Council agreed and unanimously voted to release the full payment to the contractor.

The lawyer representing Mr. Summers was himself later elected to City Council, the House of Assembly and served as Chief Justice of the Supreme Court of Newfoundland. His name was Jimmy Higgins, one of Newfoundland's most successful criminal lawyers.

BODIES EXHUMED

Headlines across the front page of the *London Daily Herald* in 1935 suggested that the Newfoundland Commission of Government was covering up the tragic and devastating affects of widespread poverty throughout Newfoundland. The story, which reported on the destitute condition of a family of eight in which two children had died while other family members struggled to live, sparked an uproar in St. John's.

The London newspaper story prompted the Newfoundland Justice Department to investigate its veracity. By this time Mrs. Roberts and four of her children had died. The Department ordered the exhumation of the bodies of all the victims. The intestines of each victim were sent to a Halifax laboratory to be analyzed. Meanwhile, the London story stated:

> Further examples of the appalling conditions under which the unemployed are living in Newfoundland are still being revealed despite Government influence to hide the facts. In many isolated settlements along Newfoundland's 6,000 mile coastline, the physical stamina of the people is cracking. The subsistence

allowance is six cents per head per day, and many of the unemployed have become ragged and weakened, and may easily become victims of diseases bred by hunger.

One of the most pitiable stories of destitution, involving the death of a girl of nine and that of a new-born baby is told by an eye-witness who helped to bury the victims. The deaths occurred on the west coast of Newfoundland about fifty miles from Corner Brook. In a wretched hut George Roberts, an unemployed man, lived on relief with his wife and six children.

All the family except the father fell ill. Neighbours state that the illnesses were caused through hunger and privation. All were suffering from dysentery. A week ago a neighbour's son visited the Roberts' home and there saw the nine-year-old girl lying helpless on the floor, while the father was staggering about the house helping the other members of the family. A neighbour then went to the house and found the girl dead. Her body was lying in rags. The mother was in bed with a baby born prematurely.

Another girl of nine was dying beside the semi-conscious mother in the same bed. Two other girls, aged two years and four years, and two boys aged six and eight were helplessly ill. They were crouched in boxes on the floor.

During pre-Confederation days, especially during the 1930s, when poverty and illness were rampant throughout Newfoundland, people often turned to home-made remedies to cure the sick. After the health of the Roberts family had deteriorated due to poor nutrition and sickness spread throughout the family, Mr. Roberts administered a home-mixed remedy of sulphur and molasses to try and cure his family. No foul play was suspected and it was believed that the sulphur contained an impurity or poison that resulted in death. Detective Walter Lee of St. John's was sent to investigate the deaths.

Soon after this tragic episode, several members of the Newfoundland Constabulary were sent for police-training in England's famous Scotland Yard. Those selected included District Inspector Whelan, Acting Sgt. Ralph Ivimey and Acting Sgt. Michael Cahill.

The Commission of Government was sometimes criticized for accumulating its $46,000,000 surplus in 1949 on the backs of the sick and poor of Newfoundland.

THE AMAZON AND THE GULLS

Ellen Broderick of Major's Path was feared by men and women alike in St. John's during the late 1800s. The following item taken from the Police Court column of the *Evening Telegram*, August 9, 1879, demonstrates why Ellen was feared. It also represents an interesting view as to how court matters were reported by the press:

> A Real amazon — Ellen Broderick, a warlike woman of twenty-five, and a denizen of Major's Path, was arraigned at the instance of John Thomas on a charge of assault and battery. The evidence failed to satisfactorily develop the actual cause of the misunderstanding, nor did it appear that Ellen was suffering from a sense of unrequited love. However, 'Nelly' and John did not love each other with as much neighbourly affection as might have been expected. The other day the quarrel waxed warm and Ellen conceived the idea of effectually putting a stop to it.

Arming herself with a formidable weapon, in the shape of a hatchet, she 'went for' John in good earnest. The latter became alarmed, and believing discretion to the better part of the valour, 'streaked' it for the chimney corner, where he snugly seated himself in close proximity to his mother's apron string, and acquainted her with the story of his marvellous escape.

Of course the old lady sympathized with him, and promised to be his protector. This morning she led him into the sacred presence, and informing his worship that she was really afraid Ellen would do him harm, begged the worthy judge to bond the said Ellen over to keep the peace. Ellen was fined, two dollars or, in default, eight days in the House of Correction.

Another Police Court column reported the appearance before the judge of an elderly St. John's lady with a city wide reputation for excessive drinking and loud behaviour. Under the heading 'Drunkenness and Vagrancy,' Margaret Bryan, 65, a resident of no particular place, got drunk and disorderly and thereby attracted the attention of the peace-makers, who speedily reduced her to a state of quietude. The Court showed mercy and discharged her without penalty.

Bill Power and his son, John, of Barter's Hill were known to the public and especially the courts as "The Gulls." The nick-names reflected their city-wide reputation for heavy drinking. Once again the newspapers had a charming way of reporting such matters as the following excerpt from the *Evening Telegram*, August 28, 1879, describes:

John Power, alias 'Little Gull,' twenty-four, fisherman, Barter's Hill, was arrested at 5 p.m. yesterday and escorted to the St. John's lock-up. He was taken into custody because he got drunk; yes, drunk. It is no unusual thing for John to 'liquor up.' The desire for 'drink' is so strong that he can't help going to the place where good men are made bad, and bad men made worse. His worship didn't detain him this morning when brought up 'for orders;' he only gave John a little wholesome admonition and then ordered him to pass out.

William Power, alias, 'Big Gull,' fifty-four, at just half-past five, followed his hopeful son, 'Gull Number One' to the headquarters of the peace-preservers. He didn't go there to see his affectionate offspring. Oh, no! He went there because he couldn't help it and whether unexpectedly or not, found himself in the same cell with the object of his paternal regard. This morning the father and son stood at the bar, charged with the same sin—drunkenness. We don't know his worship's feeling at the time, but we are inclined to believe that somebody present felt like going for "Yankee" and his contemporaries and handling them without gloves. William was discharged.

(Reference to going for 'Yankee' suggested the accused received some bruises, perhaps a black eye at the hands of the Constables).

A MEDICAL MYSTERY

The City of St. John's was faced with a medical mystery during 1938. Contagious diseases were common around Newfoundland prior to confederation and in St. John's the city medical officer gave weekly statistical reports on the problem. Some of the diseases plaguing the colony at the time included diphtheria, scarlet fever, chicken pox, tuberculosis, etc.

However, during the summer of 1938 the medical officer was perplexed over a sudden increase in contagious diseases among homes bordering on Victoria Park. The problem became serious enough for the city medical officer to launch a special medical investigation into the ordeal. His findings were shocking and provided ammunition to city councillors seeking to tighten the city plumbing regulations.

In his report to Council, the medical officer said when he visited the area he discovered raw sewerage seeping through the ground in the park. When city workers excavated the area they found that someone had hooked a rubber hose to a sewer line running through the park. The medical officer traced the hose to a private home at the top of Pleasant Street which had no water and sewerage hookup. The owner, a handy-man plumber, had devised his own sewerage removal system from his home. He placed a large coal bucket in his basement into which he dumped the daily family sewerage. He then ran the rubber hose between the coal bucket and the sewer line in the children's playground. The hose was poorly connected and leaked badly.

After the medical officer revealed the incident to council, the city took immediate action to correct the problem. A reduction in contagious diseases in the area dropped significantly. Meanwhile the City Plumber's Association succeeded in persuading council to pass regulations controlling plumbing work in St. John's.

RIOT AT HER MAJESTY'S PENITENTIARY

During March, 1945, a group of prisoners got drunk and took control of the penitentiary on Forest Road, St. John's. The situation was beyond the control of prison guards and reinforcements had to be called. However, communications were not as efficient as in later years and the warden ordered a guard to go to the fire alarm box near the prison and send in an alarm. Minutes later the fire trucks arrived and the firemen were enlisted to stand by until reinforcements could be raised from the Newfoundland Constabulary.

While authorities tried to control the trouble inside the prison, a guard was sent throughout the city to raise a posse of fifty police from around St. John's. When the police arrived the firemen returned to their stations leaving the job of putting down the riot to the police. The riot began on Sunday afternoon and it took police several hours to bring the rioters under control and to force them back into their cells.

About midnight, the police had to be called back to the prison when one of the prisoners broke out of his cell and released five or six other prisoners then gathered in one cell and challenged all. This time the police convinced them to give up quietly and return to their cells. The prisoners included Max Lush, Alf Howell, Angus Learie, Bill Power, Lew Smith, George Hussey and T. Jefferies.

The prisoners apparently made their own home brew from prunes which were part of the prison diet. The inmates gained access to the prison paint shop and stole methylated spirits. One of the prisoners had somehow gotten his hands on a master key which he used to let the other prisoners out. There were no injuries in the short-lived prison riot.

However, that same month Chief Justice Sir Edward Emerson had threatened to impose the flogging on prisoners guilty of serious crimes (physical forms of punishment). In the months before the prison riot, there had been an increase in the number of robberies with violence throughout St. John's. Emerson warned that, ". . . penalties of increasing severity would be imposed."

Justice Emerson stated, "For many years this Court has not imposed the punishment of flogging. Prisoners would realize that it is within the power of this court to order them to be flogged for certain crimes for example robbery with violence, robbery with arms or offences committed against women or children. The time seems to be approaching when judges will have to consider the conviction of this form of punishment."

A couple of years later, a prisoner named Frank DeHann broke out of one of the cells in the lock-up at the St. John's Court House. The prisoner made a key from a spoon and let himself out. He walked up the winding staircase and using his spoon-key opened the door leading into Magistrate's Court. From there he walked out to freedom. DeHann's freedom was short lived however. Several hours later he was apprehended by CID Detective Vince Noonan near the city dump at Stamp's Lane.

THE WORST KILLING

The combination of a radical religious conviction with severe mental illness caused a lighthouse keeper in northern Newfoundland to commit a barbaric killing of his favourite son. This tragic tale unfolded during the early 1960s and attracted national media attention.

Friends of the man were aware of his deep religious beliefs. He was a good father to his nine children and provided well for his family. The man knew the bible well and could quote sections of it to his friends. Neighbours did not consider he would be the type of man who would murder his own son.

Although he was responsible for the operations of a lighthouse, his family residence was in a community nearby. One day while he was loading some gas tanks from the lighthouse to take to Lewisporte to be refilled, he solicited the help of a close friend. The man agreed to help and he saw no difference in his friend's behaviour than at any time before. When he boarded the fishing boat with a tank he was startled by the sight of a small boy lying in the boat covered in blood.

The boy's father explained, "It's Terry by'. He's dead. I killed him in the will of the Lord." Terry was just four years old and his father's favourite son. The witness later told police, "At that time I saw a knife in the boat. It had blood on it." The man told his friend he had to report this to the RCMP. While he went to call the police, the killer headed home. Meanwhile, there was only one police officer available at the time and not knowing what to expect he enlisted the help of a man in the community who knew the accused killer well. When they arrived, the man had already lined up his family outdoors. He had told his wife what he had done and said it was "God's will." He then kissed the oldest boy and the youngest who was in the mother's arms.

While the police officer arrested the man the mother sobbed and said to the family friend, "I don't think it was the will of the Lord for him to kill Terry. What do you think?" The friend answered, "It's not between the covers of the book (Bible)." The accused killer was then taken by police to the Waterford Hospital to undergo a psychiatric examination. He was assessed by Dr. E.A. Moore and also observed and interviewed by Dr. D.E. Freeman, superintendent of the Waterford Hospital.

A Supreme Court jury trial was held to determine if the accused was mentally fit to stand trial. Both doctors gave testimony. Dr. Moore testified that the accused had told him why he killed the child. Dr. Moore said, "He said to me, 'I heard God's voice in the rushing wind and I offered up the boy as a sacrifice just as Abraham had done.'" When Dr. Freeman asked the accused about God's voice he explained, "I didn't hear God's voice. It came to me on the rushing wind."

The accused told the doctors that he felt he shouldn't be held at the hospital. He expressed the opinion that he would be justified in killing an attendant in order to get back home. He also added that "I had a prior right to kill my own son, but it would be wrong for me to kill another man's son."

Dr. Moore told the court that the accused clearly suffered from paranoid schizophrenia and "is under delusion or false beliefs. He is unable to distinguish between realities and unrealities." The jury found the accused unfit to stand trial for reasons of insanity and the judge sentenced him to the Waterford Hospital for an indefinite period of time.

The man who once served as head of the American Central Intelligence Agency had a close connection to Newfoundland. William Casey, in his capacity as lawyer, represented John Shaheen in negotiating the Come by Chance Oil refinery deal during the late 1960s. Casey was a powerful behind-the-scenes figure in American politics. In 1980 he served as campaign manager for former President Ronald Reagan.

According to a U.S. Senate Report in 1992, John Shaheen, along with Casey and arms dealer Cyrus Hashemi, was involved in the famous Iran-Contra, Guns for hostages deal.* Hashemi, who also handled CIA payments to Iranian officials under President Carter, was behind a $71,000,000 move by Shaheen's son Brad to regain control of the Come by Chance Refinery which had gone bankrupt in 1976.

* An unsuccessful undercover operation attempt to rescue American hostages held for over a year by Iranians. The operation was later part of an inquiry broadcast on North American television.

NEWFOUNDLAND'S MOST POWERFUL PUNCH

If there was a category for the man with the most powerful punch in Newfoundland history, it would likely go to Edward Humby who lived in Bonavista during the late nineteenth century. There were many tales of Humby's incredible strength, however the most remarkable took place in a tavern in Bonavista when a professional fighter from Philadelphia tried to show off and intimidate the local patrons.

The crew of an American fishing schooner in port had gathered at the local tavern and after some drinking were getting boisterous. One of them stood on a table and claimed to be a professional fighter. He then challenged any man in the tavern to a fight. When there was no reply he snapped, "What's the matter? Is everyone too yellow to fight?"

At this remark, Humby got to his feet. Those who knew of Humby's immense strength moved against the walls because they expected a major rumble. Humby told the American, "If it's a fight you want, I'll fight you." With that statement, he hit the huge twelve inch mortal beam, which ran across the centre of the room holding up the ceiling. The blow shook the entire tavern, and then as the wide-eyed American watched, Edward Humby struck the beam a second time. The punch shifted the support six inches out of position and drew most of the eight inch nails which connected it to the building right out of the wall.

The American got such a fright that he jumped down from the table and ran from the tavern with his friends following. Humby apologized to the tavern owner and put the beam back in place. The U.S. fishing crew showed nothing but respect for Newfoundland and Newfoundlanders during later visits. There were no arrests in the incident.

MONEY TO BURN

A Newfoundland Government employee burning garbage in an open field on the Waterford Hospital property in St.

John's in 1947 made a shocking discovery. The man was disposing of a truck-load of garbage collected from the General Post Office on Water Street. A good fire was raging and the civil servant was tossing in bag after bag of refuse when one broke open and exposed its contents: thousands of dollars! Using a pitchfork, he retrieved the burning money and put out the blaze.

He quickly brought his discovery to the attention of the authorities. The bag contained $10,000. When the item reached the media, there was speculation that there was $50,000 burned that day. This was never confirmed.

Interestingly, a year before, Detective V. Gibbons of the Newfoundland Constabulary carried out an unsuccessful investigation into a complaint that a bag of mail had been stolen from the General Post Office. Some people believed that the missing bag had contained money and had simply been misplaced among miscellaneous items in the basement of the old General Post Office. From there it got mixed in with the garbage sent for burning that day. A second possibility was that it was old currency being removed from the market for destruction and to be replaced by new bills. The mystery or crime was never solved.

GLUE-POT-FIRE ON QUEEN STREET

The fire which destroyed most of St. John's in 1846 has been called the Glue-Pot-Fire to distinguish it from the Great Fire of 1892. It was so named because it was believed that the fire had been caused by an overheated glue-pot at Hamlyn's cabinet making shop on Queen Street. Hamlyn, however, insisted that the fire had started in an apartment above his store. By the time the last cinders cooled off, 12,000 people were left homeless. Two thirds of St. John's was destroyed and property loss was estimated at $3,000,000.

The fire broke out around 8:00 a.m. on Tuesday, June 9, 1846. The fire department responded, but were unable to get their water pumps operating fast enough to stop the spreading flames. In the afternoon there were high winds that sent blazing brands, hot ash and flankers all over the city.

Governor John Harvey took a stand alongside of firemen at Beck's Cove in trying to stop the spread of flames. In an effort to create a firebreak, he ordered that the houses of Stabb, on the southwest border of the cove be blown up. During the dynamiting, an artillery man was killed by the explosion. The effort proved useless and the fire continued to spread.

By 7:00 p.m. it was all over, and the city lay in ruins. Vats of seal oil on the waterfront had exploded, spreading the fire to several ships in port. Three people lost their lives in the fire; one of them an old man trying to save his bed from a burning building. Troops were immediately dispatched to protect property and prevent looting.

Many of the homeless spent the night outdoors on Government House grounds and near Fort Townshend. As in other great calamities, people from other countries were quick to respond with help. The British Government sent 5000 pounds sterling and the British Parliament authorized another 25,000 pounds. Queen Victoria sent a letter to the Archbishop of Canterbury and York suggesting they request help from their congregations. The response was generous, and additional help came from Canada and the United States.

One of the great tragedies of that fire was the loss of many valuable historical documents and artifacts. No arrests were ever documented.

ARSON

An interesting military anecdote in St. John's involved an arson attempt at Torbay Airport. What really happened was never disclosed but there was public speculation that a member of the American military was behind the attempt. Rumours circulated throughout St. John's that a soldier had been caught red-handed with gasoline-soaked rags ready to burn Number Two Hangar. He was surprised and captured by the military police before he could do any damage. This incident followed within weeks of the destruction of Number One Hangar.

A *Sunday Herald* reporter interviewed Lieutenant Blunk, Operations Officer at Torbay, who would neither confirm nor deny the story. The reporter's investigation showed that a local pilot had put in a bill to the American authorities for 150 gallons of gasoline stolen from his private hangar.

The reporter stated, "Were this wartime, there is no doubt the intelligence would soon start suspecting subversive activity. The chain of circumstances which surround this second 'fire story' to come from Torbay Airport are so strong that the story appears true. Even the 'no comment' from American officers adds to that belief."

RUSSIAN SPYING

Red Star, the Russian Army magazine, displayed seven pictures of American Army bases in Newfoundland taken shortly after World War II. The photo-display included two pictures of Fort Pepperrell, St. John's; two of Gander, one of Argentia, and two of Harmon Field, Stephenville. It would have been easy to get a picture of Gander, but no pictures of military bases were permitted. Canadian authorities could not explain how the Russians obtained their pictures. There was speculation that Russian agents had obtained pictures either directly or indirectly from sources on the island. The pictures showed landing strips at Harmon, warehouses at Argentia, hospital facilities at Fort Pepperrell and the entrance gates to the bases.

Soon after North Americans became aware of the magazine pictures, the United States tightened security at its Newfoundland bases.

RNC CAPTURED ENEMY SHIP

A decision by the captain of a Finnish ship had unexpected consequences for him and an encounter with the Newfoundland Constabulary. The story happened soon after England declared war on Finland during WWII and remained unknown until after the war. Although the United States had bases in Newfoundland, the Americans had not at the time declared war on Finland. A Finnish ship in Newfoundland waters sought refuge at Argentia because its captain assumed Argentia would be a neutral port.

A police officer at Argentia heard that the Fin_n
was heading for Argentia and he called the Con_st
at St. John's. The local police armed thirty offic_e
tommy guns and obtained a small ship to take   t
Argentia.

The Constabulary intercepted the Fins jus_t
Argentia Harbour. The captain and crew of the_
vessel were shocked when the Newfoundlanders   c
board branding weapons and took control of the_e
The Fins were made prisoners of war. They were   _ke
Placentia jail and were later turned over to the m_ili

KNIGHTS OF COLUMBUS MYSTERY SOLVED

The Newfoundland Constabulary, the   _Du
Commission and the American Counter Int_elli
Organization all investigated the tragic fire at the   K
of Columbus in St. John's on December 12, 194_2_.
none of these investigations solved the crime, al_ c
ered that a pyromaniac may have been at work_.
inevitable that in the midst of a world war there _vo
strong speculation that the arson which killed nin_ety
people was the work of enemy agents. As years tur_ne
decades, the enemy agent theory strengthened, f_uel
rumours and the realization that there were peop_le
K of C that night who remained missing. One   _of
missing was said to have been a German agent. An_on
rumours that enhanced the enemy agent theory w_as t
man who had died mysteriously at the K of C   mo
before the fire may have stumbled onto some   kin

enemy plot. My own research into this claim disclosed the following incident which may have sparked such a rumour.

MURDER OR ACCIDENT

During April 1942, nine months before the Knights of Columbus tragedy, Mrs. Annie Barron, housekeeper at the Knights of Columbus made an unnerving discovery in the basement of the building. Mrs. Barron began her duties around 9:00 a.m. on April 17, 1942. She went to the basement and unlocked the door to the laundry. After entering she was startled to see two feet extending from beneath some shelving. The rest of the body was buried among soiled linen.

Mrs. Barron rushed back up the stairs and reported her finding to Mr. M.J. Quinn, the K of C Manager. Quinn immediately called in the police. Within minutes three police officers arrived followed by Dr. Anderson and Dr. Josephson. The area was investigated and the body taken to the city morgue for examination. The victim was identified as James 'Jimmy' Love, a Scottish seaman whose ship had been torpedoed several weeks before.

The constabulary concluded that the victim had accidentally fallen down the laundry shute from the first floor to the basement and had suffered a fractured skull which caused his death. The laundry room where the victim was found extended from the basement to the top story — a distance of fifteen feet. The opening from the top floor was through a hatch in the floor. Police concluded Mr. Love had fallen through the opening to his death in the basement laundry room.

Dr. Josephson reported that, based on the condition of the body, the victim had been dead several days before he was discovered by Annie Barron. Conspiracy theories hatched easily and for years after the K of C fire, people whispered about a soldier connected to the arson having been murdered and his body shoved down a laundry shute. Neither Newfoundland authorities nor American Army Intelligence even referred to the incident in their investigations and no connection with the tragedy was ever officially recognized.

GERMAN AGENT OR CANADIAN SOLDIER

One of the most dominant theories to what may have happened, and one which became part of the oral history associated with the mystery, was that one of the entertainers at the K of C that night was the arsonist. It was claimed that Hector Wooley of the Royal Canadian Navy was actually a German spy who had assumed the identity of Wooley after illegally entering the country.

According to the story, Wooley set the fire and was eventually captured. He was then tried in a military court at Fort Pepperrell and executed there before a firing squad. To avoid public panic, the story goes on to claim that the matter was classified as top-secret and kept from the public. This theory was given credibility by the claim that Wooley was missing and presumed dead. The Dunfield Report listed him missing. Press reports over the years claimed he was missing and presumed dead. Engraved on the K of C Memorial on Harvey Road, along with thirteen others, he is recorded as missing and presumed dead.

In an effort to clear up the mystery, I obtained a copy of the U.S. Counter-Intelligence Investigation Report. The conclusion drawn by the Americans paralleled those of the Dunfield Commission: "There was no evidence as to who started it and no evidence of German involvement." There is nothing in either the Dunfield or the American investigation to suggest in any way that Wooley was involved in the tragedy.

While researching the Wooley Theory, I learned that Wooley and ten others who had been listed as missing and presumed dead were not missing at all. All had died in the fire and are buried in cemeteries here in St. John's. All had properly marked tombstones which indicate the date of death as December 12, 1942.

THE ANSWER

After the publication of my book *Newfoundland Disasters*, which includes the Knights of Columbus tragedy, I was approached by Bren Walsh, author and retired CBC broadcaster then living in the United States. Bren told me that he was pursuing the idea of doing a book on war time anecdotes. He said that he requested and obtained an interview with an Adjutant-General at the Pentagon in Washington regarding the K of C fire.

He informed me that the AG had on his desk a file which he referred to during the interview. Bren learned from the AG that the American military had solved the mystery and had made an arrest. According to Bren, the AG gave him the name of the K of C arsonist, and said that the arsonist had been tried in an American court and had served his time in an American military prison. I was doing a Newfoundland radio show at that time and Bren asked me to refrain from using the story until he was ready to release it. I believe he intended to use it in his planned book. Soon after, Bren passed away and his findings were never published.

Knights of Columbus building in St. John's c. 1942

Almost ten years later I made an extensive but unsuccessful effort to confirm Bren's story. The Army Counter-Intelligence Report, which was carried out in 1943, had nothing in it to suggest the crime had been solved. However, I considered the possibility that the crime may have been solved after that report had been completed. I then sought to trace the person allegedly convicted for the arson through the U.S. military prison system records. The National Archives in Washington directed me to the U.S. Army Criminal Investigation Command in Virginia. I was advised by Wilbur Hardy, Director of Crime Records at CIC that, ". . . records located at this centre are retained for a period of forty years, after which, they are destroyed."

Both the Dunfield Enquiry and the American Army Intelligence had suggested it may have been the work of a pyromaniac. Certainly there were many other fires and arson attempts around St. John's at the time to support the theory that the K of C was burned by a pyromaniac. Without the benefit of Bren Walsh's records regarding the crime and considering the man served his time in a U.S. prison, it is reasonable to conclude that the arson was the work of a pyromaniac who was an American soldier.

Supporting this conclusion is two little known arsons that took place on American property the same year as the K of C fire. About eight months before the K of C tragedy, one of the American barracks on the base at St. John's was set ablaze. The fire broke out at 9:00 p.m. on February 1, 1942, and the American firemen were unable to contain it. Firefighters from St. John's were called in and by midnight had totally quenched the fire. Like the K of C fire, it was also set between the roof and the ceiling.

On December 1, 1942, an arsonist destroyed an American barracks on Signal Hill near the Battery. Residents of the Battery had to be evacuated. The structure was built near the side of a cliff and almost inaccessible to fire fighters. Once again the military fire fighting team could not control the fire and turned to firemen from St. John's to battle the flames. It was a dangerous battle because the city firemen had to lash down their two water pumpers with rope on the precipice of a cliff and pump water from St. John's Harbour. The building was destroyed but firefighters prevented the fire from spreading to nearby houses at the Battery. Other arson attempts during that period included the USO Building on Merrymeeting Road and the Red Triangle on Water Street (in both cases the arsonist used similar methods as at the K of C). There was also a fire at the Old Colony — a popular club for the military during the war years.